KT-481-328

CONTENTS

THERE'S ALWAYS ONE CLOWN...

HORRIBLE GEOGRAPHY

ODIOUS OCEANS

ANITA GANERI ILLUSTRATED BY MIKE PHILLIPS

Also available
Bloomin' Rainforests · Cracking Coasts · Desperate Deserts ·
Earth-Shattering Earthquakes · Freaky Peaks · Monster Lakes ·
Perishing Poles · Raging Rivers · Stormy Weather ·
Violent Volcanoes · Wild Islands

Horrible Geography Handbooks
Planet in Peril
Wicked Weather
Wild Animals

Specials
Intrepid Explorers
Horrible Geography of the World

Scholastic Children's Books,
Euston House, 24 Eversholt Street,
London, NW1 1DB, UK

A division of Scholastic Ltd
London ~ New York ~ Toronto ~ Sydney ~ Auckland
Mexico City ~ New Delhi ~ Hong Kong

First published in the UK by Scholastic Ltd, 1999
This edition published by Scholastic Ltd, 2008

Text copyright © Anita Ganeri, 1999
Illustrations copyright © Mike Phillips, 1999, 2008

ISBN 978 0439 94454 0
All rights reserved

Printed in the UK by CPI Bookmarque, Croydon

10 9 8 7

THERE'S
ALWAYS ONE
CLOWN...

HORRIBLE GEOGRAPHY

ODIOUS OCEANS

ANITA GANERI ILLUSTRATED BY MIKE PHILLIPS

Also available
Bloomin' Rainforests • Cracking Coasts • Desperate Deserts •
Earth-Shattering Earthquakes • Freaky Peaks • Monster Lakes •
Perishing Poles • Raging Rivers • Stormy Weather •
Violent Volcanoes • Wild Islands

Horrible Geography Handbooks
Planet in Peril
Wicked Weather
Wild Animals

Specials
Intrepid Explorers
Horrible Geography of the World

Scholastic Children's Books,
Euston House, 24 Eversholt Street,
London, NW1 1DB, UK

A division of Scholastic Ltd
London ~ New York ~ Toronto ~ Sydney ~ Auckland
Mexico City ~ New Delhi ~ Hong Kong

First published in the UK by Scholastic Ltd, 1999
This edition published by Scholastic Ltd, 2008

Text copyright © Anita Ganeri, 1999
Illustrations copyright © Mike Phillips, 1999, 2008

ISBN 978 0439 94454 0
All rights reserved

Printed in the UK by CPI Bookmarque, Croydon

10 9 8 7

The right of Anita Ganeri and Mike Phillips to be identified as the author and illustrator of this work respectively has been asserted by them in accordance with the Copyright, Designs and Patents Act, 1988.

INTRODUCTION

Geography. It's a horrible word, isn't it? And what on Earth does it mean? Is it all about boring old rivers in boring old valleys in boring old countries you can't even spell? The answer is yes, it's all these things, but it's a whole lot more besides. Don't let your teacher go into details. The horrible truth about geography teachers is that they never know when to stop.

So what do geographers actually do? Try this experiment. Stare out of the window and have a good look outside. Look harder. What can you see? A clump of trees? Some clouds in the sky? A rolling field? The road into town? (The dog digging up your mum's prize dahlias?)

* That's the posh name for a huge wave which rushes up a river from the sea with the incoming tide. And NOTHING TO DO WITH TEACHERS!

Congratulations! You're a geographer. Why? Well, geography is actually made up of two old Greek words which mean "the science of describing the world". And that's what you've been doing. (The dog won't get off so lightly!)

But geography can also be horribly misleading. Take calling our planet "Earth", for example. Not a very clever way to describe a place that's covered in far more water than land. Far better to call it planet "Ocean". The oceans are the biggest places on the planet by far. And the awesome odious oceans are what this book is all about.

In *Odious Oceans*, you can...

- dive down to the deepest depths with Dirk, the deep–sea diver.

(* Posh term for a geographer who studies the sea.)

- learn to love a great white shark (you can do it!).

- find out why the *Titanic* really sank.
- see if you've got what it takes to join up with the Navy. You'll never think geography's boring again.

GOING DOWN

A journey to the bottom of the sea (almost)

On the morning of 23 January 1960, at 8.15 am on the dot, two men smiled nervously, said goodbye to their shipmates and entered a tiny steel capsule hanging beneath a huge, cigar-shaped tank.

They were about to embark on the voyage of their lives, and earn a place in the geography books. The capsule was only the size of a small car, and packed with so much equipment that there was barely space for the men to sit down. But then no one had said it was going to be a comfortable ride. Slowly, the ship's crane heaved and groaned into action and lowered the capsule overboard, into the dark waters of the Pacific Ocean. The two men shook hands and wished each other luck. Their descent into the unknown had begun...

The two men were scientists, Dr Jacques Piccard and Lieutenant Don Walsh of the US Navy. Their extraordinary craft was called *Trieste*. Technically, it was known as a bathyscaphe (bath-ee-scafe), like a mini-submarine. The scientists' mission was to dive to the bottom of the Challenger Deep, in the monstrous Marianas Trench, a gigantic gash in the seabed, and the deepest spot known on the planet. *No one had ever tried this before. No one even knew if you could.*

Piccard and Walsh sat anxiously in cramped silence as *Trieste* sank down through the dark icy waters, waiting for their echo-sounder to warn them that they were nearing the bottom.

They knew only too well how fraught with danger their journey was. But neither knew what lay beneath them. Or if *Trieste* would stand the strain. And that wasn't all. All that separated them from the crushing weight or pressure of the water above them (imagine having a lorry balanced on your thumbnail) was the capsule's thick, steel walls. At about 9,000 metres, they put on the brakes to slow *Trieste*'s descent – a crash landing would be disastrous. Suddenly, there was a sickening CRAACKK!

"What on earth was that?" said Piccard, looking round nervously.

For a moment, their hearts were in their mouths ... but it was a false alarm. One of *Trieste*'s outer windows had cracked under the tremendous weight of the water. But the capsule itself stayed watertight. The men breathed a huge sigh of relief. Then came the moment they had been waiting for ... and dreading. At 1.06 pm, a nail-biting four hours and 48 minutes after leaving the surface, *Trieste* bumped and grated along the silty bottom of the Challenger Deep and came to a juddering halt.

Hearts thumping, Piccard and Walsh switched on their floodlights, and peered into a world no one had ever seen before – the deepest, darkest depths of the oceans. And from somewhere in that eerie darkness, something was staring back. But that was impossible – nothing could live this far down! There wasn't enough oxygen in the water for anything to survive. Surely? Not for the first time, or for the last, science was to be proved wrong. The staring something was a ghostly white flat fish a bit like a flounder. And it was very much alive. Soon afterwards, a small, reddish creature, shaped like a shrimp, also went scuttling past.

Teeth chattering with cold, Piccard and Walsh spent 20 minutes on the seabed, munching on chocolate bars for nourishment. Then, releasing two tonnes of iron-pellet ballast which had kept *Trieste* weighted down, they began their slow, steady ascent, breaking the surface at 4.56 pm, three hours and 17 minutes later.

Their journey of 22 kilometres had taken eight and a half hours. They had dived to a depth of almost 11 kilometres, deeper than anyone else ... before or since. Piccard and Walsh's amazing record still stands today, as the deepest dive ever made. And one of the greatest feats of ocean exploration ever.

THE ODIOUS OCEANS

While exploring the odious oceans in a mini–sub might be way out of your depth, there are plenty of much safer ways of getting to know them better. But, wait a minute, don't plunge in just yet, there are a couple of things you'll need to know about oceans first. For example:

- where on Earth are they?
- what on Earth are they?
- why on Earth are they there in the first place? (OK, so that's three things, but who's counting?)

Look at the map opposite for starters.

As you can see, oceans are absolutely HUGE. They're also hugely wet and salty. And full of extraordinary plants and animals. Actually, the oceans are so odiously vast, that there are still hundreds of kilometres of silty seabed which no one has ever seen ... yet. In fact, until recently, geographers thought that most of the seabed was just boringly sandy and flat. (Of course, none of them had been there, so none of them really knew. And they had to say something.) Now we know that there are high mountains, plunging valleys, active volcanoes, rumbling earthquakes, rolling plains – you get the picture – all covered up by the water. Awesome.

Fascinating facts about the odious oceans

1 The odious oceans cover two-thirds of the Earth. Like we said before, they're big! And over half of this water is in just one ocean – the Pacific. Next in order of size come the Atlantic, Indian, Southern and Arctic oceans. For most of the year, the f-f-freezing Arctic Ocean is covered in a thick sheet of ice with the North Pole stuck in the middle. The Southern Ocean is icy too but that's the least of its problems. Some horrible geographers say it doesn't exist! They claim

that it's part of the Atlantic, Indian and Pacific oceans and not an odious ocean in its own right. Spoilsports.

2 Your teachers may tell you that the sea is blue. Don't believe a word of it. The sea only looks blue on sunny days when the water reflects blue light rays from the sun. The rest of the time it looks greenish or grey. The greener the sea, the better, because this means that...

By the way, some seas aren't green, grey, or blue. The White Sea is white because it's covered in ice. And, very occasionally the Red Sea gets so chock-full of tiny red plants (another type of appetizing algae) that it takes on a pinky tinge.

3 The oceans are about 4,000 million years old (even older than your grandparents). Not long before they came along,

the Earth formed from a cloud of dust and gas. As it cooled and solidified, water vapour (that's water in gas form) rose into the air from violent volcanoes on the surface. The vapour cooled and formed storm clouds, and torrential rain poured and filled the first oceans with water.

THE OCEANS BEGIN TO FILL

4 The very first oceans weren't great places for holidays. Forget warm, salty water and long, sandy beaches. The water was boiling hot, with a bitter taste like vinegar. Today it's salty because, well, it's got salt in it. Just like the stuff you put on your chips.

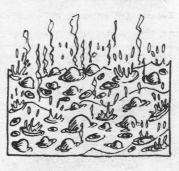

Some of this comes from undersea volcanoes. Some falls in the rain. Most comes from rocks on land, washed into the sea by rivers. And there's plenty of it. Enough, in fact, to cover the Earth with a layer 150 metres thick.

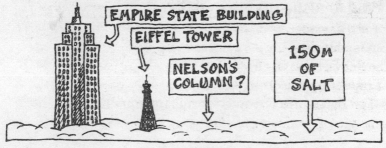

EMPIRE STATE BUILDING
EIFFEL TOWER
NELSON'S COLUMN?
150M OF SALT

5 The geographical name for common old saltiness is salinity. To be horribly technical, it's measured as the number of parts of salt in one thousand parts of water. This is measured as p.s.u. (practical salinity units). The more salt in the sea, the better you float.

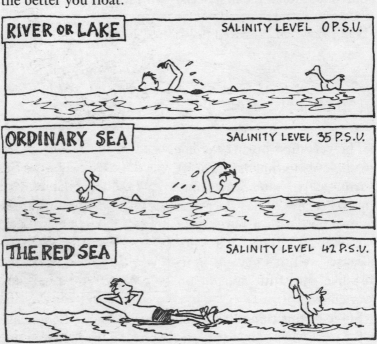

RIVER OR LAKE — SALINITY LEVEL 0 P.S.U.

ORDINARY SEA — SALINITY LEVEL 35 P.S.U.

THE RED SEA — SALINITY LEVEL 42 P.S.U.

Try this simple taste test.

How to rustle up the Red Sea
You will need:
some salt
some warm water
a bucket or measuring jug
a few drops of red food colouring (optional)

What to do:
- Put four level teaspoons of salt into a litre of water.
- Stir until all the salt dissolves.
- Add a few drops of red food colouring. (This *is* the Red Sea, remember.)
- Take a sip (just a small one).
That's how salty the Red Sea is!

6 Some funny things have happened in the history of the oceans. About 6.5 million years ago, the Mediterranean Sea became completely cut off from the odious Atlantic. One thousand years later, the sea water had all dried up in the sun, leaving the seabed caked in salt a kilometre thick. Eventually the sea level rose again in the Atlantic and a gigantic waterfall splashed over the Straits of Gibraltar (that's the channel that joins the Atlantic and Med) and poured into the Mediterranean. Even so it took roughly 100 years for the Mediterranean to fill up again.

7 It's a bit misleading to call the sea "level". Like everything else, it has its ups and downs. During the last Ice Age, 18,000 years ago, so much water was locked up in glaciers, that the sea level dropped by 100 metres. Enough to make it possible to walk from England to France – if you'd got a couple of days to spare. Since then, it's risen about ten centimetres every 100 years. Geographers know how sea levels have risen in the last 5,000 years because they've found the bones and teeth of land-living mammals, like mammoths and horses, in the seabed. They all drowned when the sea level rose.

CHANGES IN WORLD WIDE SEA LEVELS ARE CALLED 'EUSTATIC' CHANGES, I'M NOT TOO ECSTATIC ABOUT THEM MY SELF!

FRANCE

Teacher teaser

Just how in-depth is your teacher's geography? Scratch your head as if you're deep in thought and ask:

PLEASE, SIR, HOW HEAVY IS THE SEA?

Answer: The water in the sea weighs an incredible 1.2 QUINTILLION tonnes! That's 1,200,000,000,000,000,000 tonnes. And that's just for starters. The deeper you go, the heavier it feels. This is called water pressure. In the deepest ocean, the water pressure is like having 20 elephants sitting on top of you. Ouch!

Earth-shattering fact
Once upon a time, people believed that the Earth was flat. They thought that if you sailed too far in one direction, you'd fall off the edge and end up in Hell! An even more Earth-shattering fact is that some people still think this.

Some salty seas

Did you know that some parts of the oceans aren't called oceans at all? They're seas. To make matters worse, some seas aren't really seas, but salty lakes. As a rule, a real sea is a part of an ocean. So the South China Sea is part of the Pacific Ocean and the North Sea is part of the Atlantic Ocean. Confused? Try dipping your toes into these salty seas:

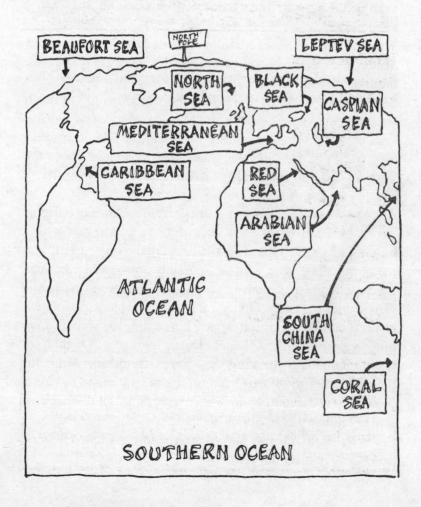

Black Sea The ancient Greeks called this "the hospitable sea", even though it was horribly rocky and stormy. They thought that it was unlucky to give a thing a bad name, however nasty it actually turned out to be. Later the Turks changed the sea's name because it scared them to death!

Dead Sea This sea is called "dead" because its water's so salty nothing can live in it for long. It's five times saltier than most of the oceans. But it's not really a sea at all. It's a salty, inland lake.

Mediterranean Sea The Romans called the Mediterranean Sea the "sea at the centre of the Earth". Because they really thought it was.

Seven Seas Ancient sailors used the word "seven" to mean "many". And "many" meant the only seas they knew, a grand total of seven. These were the Red Sea, the Mediterranean Sea, the Persian Gulf, the Black Sea, the China Sea, the Caspian Sea and the Indian Ocean. In fact, there are more like 70 seas than seven. But they didn't care.

Aegean Sea This sea was named after an ancient king of Athens, called Aegeus, who according to legend met with a rather sticky end. This is how it happened. King Aegeus had a son, called Theseus, who was horribly brave and handsome. Already, by the tender age of ten, he'd killed several gruesome giants and monsters. They included the painfully-named giant, Pine-bender, who strapped his victims to two bent-over pine trees, then, all of a sudden, let the trees go ... Ouch! Now he set off on his greatest test yet – to kill the hideous Minotaur (half-man, half-bull) that lived on the nearby island of Crete. Nobody else dared to go anywhere near him. But this show of bravery didn't please Theseus's dad.

"Why can't you just stay at home and get married?" he said. "Like a nice, normal boy."

"No way," replied Theseus. (He could be stubborn, too.)

"Oh all right," Aegeus sighed. "You win. But if you do kill the Minotaur, instead of the other way round, please, please, please change your sails from black to white as you sail home. Then I'll know you're safe."

"No problem, Dad," said Theseus, not really listening. "See you later."

To cut a long story short, Theseus reached Crete, and proved himself brave enough to kill the Minotaur and handsome enough to get himself engaged to Ariadne, daughter of the King of Crete. She'd fancied him for ages and ages. She sailed home with Theseus to meet his mum and dad. On the way back, the two love-birds stopped at the island of Naxos for the night. But while Ariadne was fast asleep, Theseus sailed off and left her. Just like that. No note, no nothing.

When Ariadne woke up and found herself abandoned, she was FURIOUS.

Luckily, she had friends in high places, including a god, called Dionysus. (He fancied Ariadne.) He played a trick on Theseus and made him forget his promise. You remember, the one about changing his sails? So, Theseus sailed off home, without a care, black sails a-blazing. What a mistake! Thinking him dead, poor old Aegeus went mad with grief, leapt off a cliff into the sea and was drowned. So Athens lost a king but gained a name for a sea.

THE DAILY GLOBE

GHASTLY GOINGS-ON DOWN UNDER

What is the deep seabed really like? Is it really deeply dull, boring and flat? Or are the rumours of mountains, volcanoes and valleys actually true? Is the deep sea floor all it's cracked up to be? We at *The Daily Globe* were determined to get to the bottom of things. So we sent our roving reporter, C. Shanty, on a special, record-breaking assignment...

Underwater mountain bigger than Everest shock!

It's official! Everest is not the highest mountain on Earth. At a paltry 8,848 metres, Everest is over ONE KILOMETRE (that's 1,000 metres) shorter than majestic Mauna Kea.

MAUNA KEA

EVEREST

This gigantic volcano in the Pacific Ocean rises an astonishing 10,203 metres from the sea floor. And that's a world record. The tip of the mountain breaks the surface of the sea and sprouts into a heavenly Hawaiian island. As you can see, while I was there, I took some time off to explore…

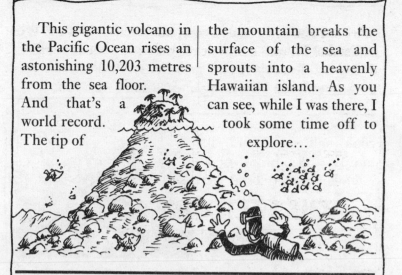

Spreading ridges – is the Atlantic cracking up?

Back on the job, I set sail for the middle of the Atlantic Ocean. Under this ocean, so I'm told, runs the world's longest mountain chain. Straight down the middle, all the way from Iceland (where you can see it sticking out of the sea) to Antarctica lies the boringly named Mid-Atlantic Ridge. It's over 11,000 km long, with mountains 4 km tall. In most places it lies a whopping 2 km underwater.

WET BIT

DRY BIT

MID-ATLANTIC RIDGE

OVER 11,000 KM LONG AND 4 KM HIGH

To tell you the truth, it's not as boring as it sounds. All along the ridge, red-hot, runny rock seeps up through cracks in the seabed. As it hits the water, cools and goes solid, it builds up brand-new mountains and volcanoes.

And, clever old ridge, it also makes new seabed. At the last count, the Atlantic was getting wider each year, by a whole four cm! Geographers call this "seafloor spreading". Because, er, it's the seafloor and, well, it's spreading … but I didn't have time to wait around to watch.

Hitting the depths in the murky Marianas

Next, to the north-west Pacific and the murky Marianas Trench. This place holds the record for the deepest, darkest place on Earth. And the spookiest, take it from me.

But it's not the only trench in the sea. A trench is a huge, ghastly gash in the sea floor, which happens when one piece of seabed is pushed under another and melts back into the Earth. This is called subduction, a posh way of saying pushing under. And it's just as well it happens. Trenches balance out seafloor spreading and stop the Earth getting bigger and bigger. Imagine the chaos that would cause! I'd never get back to the office. Come to think of it…

The Marianas Trench is a staggering 11,034 metres

deep. Lose your flipper down there, and it'll take ONE WHOLE HOUR to reach the bottom! Luckily, I kept my flippers firmly on my feet.

Top secret – dead bodies litter ocean floor

They cover over half the sea floor, stretching for kilometres on end. They're flatter than anywhere on land. They're the truly abysmal abyssal plains. But it's not their flatness that makes the hairs on your neck stand on end. These awful places are covered in a ghastly carpet of ooze, made from the bodies of billions and billions of minuscule sea creatures which have rained down from the surface. Billions of DEAD sea creatures.

I'm outta here!

Who boasts the most coast?

Back on land (phew!) the coastlines can break a few records too. Did you know that if all the world's coastlines were straightened out, they'd stretch round the Earth 13 times? Congratulations, Canada! Not only are you one of the world's largest countries but with over 90,000 km of seashore, you can also boast the most coast. In second place is Indonesia, with a paltry 47,000 km.

CANADA: SOME GREAT WIGGLY BITS

And finally, you will need to fly south to the north coast of Hawaii to find the world's highest sea cliffs. Dive over the edge and you've a whole kilometre to fall before you finally reach the sea. You wouldn't catch me getting too close to the edge. Which is precisely why I'm finishing this report from the safety of the lounge in the Ocean View Hotel. Cheers!

CHEERS!

A moving story

Ever fancied a house by the sea? Sounds great, doesn't it, but in fact it can be horribly tough living along the coast, what with the wind, waves and weather constantly pounding against the shore and eating away at the rocks and cliffs. This is called erosion, and it doesn't half grind you down. The way waves crash into the shore is called "breaking". Here's what happens:

How to ride a breaking wave

What you will need:
a seashore
a surfboard
a willing victim (actually, the willing bit's not essential)

What to do:
We've asked Dirk the deep-sea diver to show you the ropes:
1 The wave starts off smooth and low. So far, so good.

TOO SLOW FOR AN EXPERT LIKE ME

2 As it nears the shore, it slows down because of friction*
with the sea floor.**

THIS IS MORE LIKE IT

(*Friction is a force which tries to stop things moving past each other. Try sliding your fingertips along your desk. Friction makes them harder and harder to move.)
(**Oceanographers call this "feeling the bottom". But that's quite enough of that. Snigger.)

3 It gets steeper and taller…

4 …until it topples over and breaks on the shore. Aaaaghh!

Making waves

Because of waves and currents, the odious oceans are constantly on the move. But what on Earth are they? Waves are made by the wind blowing across the surface of the sea. The stronger the wind, the bigger the waves. And some can be horribly huge. In 1933, the unfortunate crew of a ship called USS *Ramapo* had the fright of their lives when a wave, measuring 34 metres high (that's higher than a ten-storey building), reared its ugly head in front of them. Luckily, they lived to tell the tale.

THEY HAD GOOD REASON TO BE RATTLED. WAVES ARE INCREDIBLY STRONG. IN 1968 A GIGANTIC WAVE HIT AN OIL TANKER OFF THE COAST OF AFRICA, AND SNAPPED THE SHIP CLEAN IN TWO!

If you want to go out in rough weather, it's probably safest to travel by submarine. Waves only ruffle the surface of the water, so if you're deep enough down, you won't feel a thing.

Try making some waves of your own. They'll be a bit smaller than the real thing, of course. Fill a bowl with water and blow across the surface. Remember, the harder you blow, the bigger the waves. Go on, blow harder! If your mum tells you off for making a mess, look shocked and say:

BUT MUM, I WAS JUST STUDYING SIMPLE OSCILLATIONS!

THAT'S "WAVES" TO YOU AND ME

Troublesome tidal waves

Tidal waves are:

a) not really waves at all (because they aren't caused by the wind) and

b) nothing to do with tides.

They're triggered off by earthquakes or volcanoes deep beneath the sea. These send shock waves quivering through the water which make it bulge and ripple. At first, the ripples aren't much to look at – in fact, they can pass ships by without anyone noticing. But they're speedy movers, racing along as fast as jet planes, until they reach the land. Then the trouble really starts. They rear up over 30 metres high, and crash down again with a mighty SPLASH!

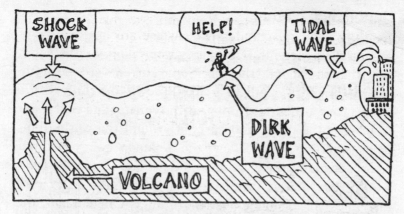

One type of tidal wave contains enough water to drown a whole island. Geographers call these waves tsunamis (soo-naa-mees), a Japanese word meaning "harbour waves". The largest ever was 85 metres high. In 1946, a tsunami in Hawaii picked up a house, carried it a few hundred metres down the road and put it down again. So gently that the breakfast plates were still on the table!

Undercover currents

Swirling about just under the surface are huge rivers of water called currents. These are swept along by the wind. But what on Earth do they do? Some currents are warm (up to a sizzling 30°C); others are cold (down to a chilly -2°C). They take warm water from near the equator and cold water from near the poles, and carry it around the world. This helps to heat up and cool down the land more evenly. Without crucial currents, the equator would get hotter, and the poles would get colder. And that would make life very uncomfortable. Some currents are huge. One current, the chilly West Wind Drift, flows around Antarctica, carrying 2,000 times more water than the mighty Amazon River in Brazil, the largest river in the world!

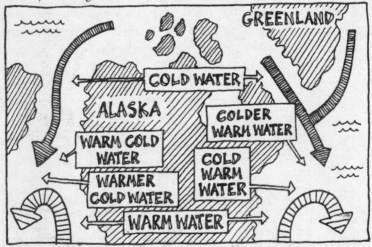

Tricky tides

It's not just waves or currents that keep the oceans in non-stop motion. Twice a day, the sea rises and floods on to the seashore. And twice a day, it flows out again. The posh word for this is "ebbing". These changes are called the tides. High tide is when the water is in. Low tide's when it's out again. Tides are mainly caused by the moon's gravity pulling the oceans nearest to it into a giant bulge. But that's not all. While all this is going on, the Earth is spinning on its axis (an imaginary line running down its middle). And as it spins, it pulls the oceans on the other side into another bulge. Confused? Don't be. See Dirk's deep-sea diagram No. 1.

Dirk's deep-sea diagram No. 1

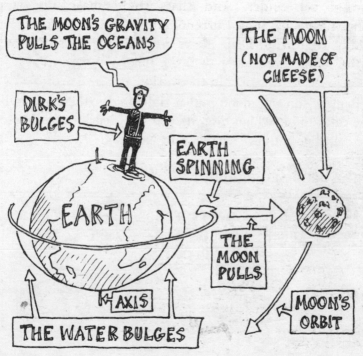

To muddle matters more, twice a month the sun gets in on the action. When the sun and moon pull in a straight line, they cause very high high-waters and very low low-waters. These are called spring tides. See deep-sea diagram No. 2.

Dirk's deep-sea diagram No. 2

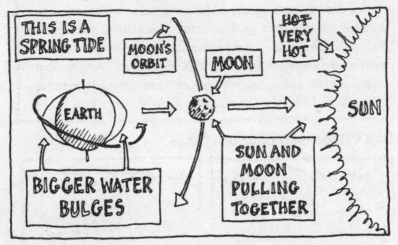

This is a spring tide

Moon's orbit

Moon

Hot very hot

Earth

Sun

Bigger water bulges

Sun and moon pulling together

When the sun and moon pull at right angles, there are high low tides and low high tides. If you see what I mean. These are called neap tides. See diagram No. 3.

Dirk's deep-sea diagram No. 3

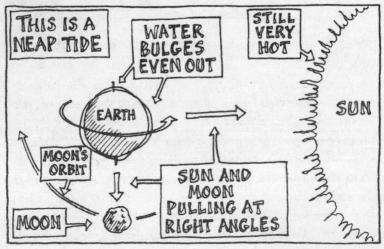

This is a neap tide

Water bulges even out

Still very hot

Earth

Sun

Moon's orbit

Moon

Sun and moon pulling at right angles

Dirk's deep-sea diagram No. 4

The Bermuda Triangle or There are three parts to every story

One particularly perilous part of the oceans is the baffling Bermuda Triangle. It's a huge, triangular stretch of the Atlantic Ocean, between Puerto Rico, Miami and Bermuda. And it's been puzzling geographers for years. Why? Well, in the last 40 years, the troublesome Triangle has swallowed up at least 100 ships and hundreds of unfortunate sailors. Never to be seen again.

For example, in 1918, a huge great coal ship, called *Cyclops* vanished without trace while crossing the Triangle, with all

309 of its crew. But the trouble started long before that. In 1881, one ship, carrying a cargo of timber, lost three crews in a week, before disappearing altogether! In most cases, ships disappear in calm weather, for no apparent reason. And they vanish so fast that they don't have time to send out an SOS.

And it's not just ships. Picture the scene. It's 5 December 1944. The Second World War is raging. Five US Navy torpedo bombers, each with a three-man crew, are flying over the sea en route from Florida. One by one, as they cross the Triangle, they vanish into thin air... The day is clear and sunny. Their instruments are working perfectly. A rescue plane is dispatched to find them. Within minutes, it too has disappeared!

What on Earth is going on? Is it coincidence, or something more sinister? Who or what is to blame? Here are some possible culprits:

1 The weather in this part of the Atlantic can be awfully unpredictable. You can have blue skies one minute and a howling gale the next. The worst sorts of storm are hurricanes. These tropical terrors can blow ships off course or smash them to smithereens.

2 Ships might also be sunk by waterspouts. These are swirling funnels of air. They hang down from storm clouds over the sea. When the swirling air touches down on the water, the water is sucked up by the air to make a huge column of spray. These columns can be over a kilometre tall. But waterspouts only hang about for 10 to15 minutes. After that you'd need to DUCK!, as all that water comes crashing back down.

3 What about massive underwater explosions? Could they hold the key? In 1995, scientists discovered a huge build-up of methane gas under the seabed. One scientist said:

RELEASING THIS GAS WOULD BE LIKE SHAKING AN ENORMOUS CAN OF POP. THE OCEAN WOULD FIZZ UP AND SHIPS LOSE ALL BUOYANCY AND SINK WITHOUT A TRACE IN MINUTES. WATER CONTAINING HUGE AMOUNTS OF GAS IS LESS DENSE THAN NORMAL, SO BOATS WOULD SINK AND PLANES PLUMMET.

(PS There'd also be a terrible pong – methane smells awful!)

4 Metal that's formed underneath the ocean floor could act like a massive magnet. Something certainly confuses ships' compasses in the triangle. And this might cause them to sail in the wrong direction and get hopelessly lost!

A COMPASS NEEDLE USUALLY POINTS TOWARDS MAGNETIC NORTH, NOT THE NORTH POLE. BUT IN THE TREACHEROUS TRIANGLE IT CAN POINT TO BOTH.

5 And why is the wreckage never found? Well, that might have something to do with odious ocean currents. The surging Gulf Stream can carry debris far away before the search team can find it. Small whirlpools, called eddies, help to scatter the wreckage.

6 Once under water, debris is also quickly buried by sand or silt on the sea floor. On the other hand, it could be sucked into a "blue hole", whatever that is!

As for lost crews, their bodies are quite probably gobbled up by sharks.

What do you think? At least these theories sound as if they could be true. Which is more than can be said for others. Some people claim that ships entering the Triangle are snatched by aliens in flying saucers who use the sailors in extraterrestrial experiments. Weird.

If all this mystery has made you peckish (it affects some people like that), don't worry. You won't have to wait very long for a snack. The next chapter is crammed full of mouth-watering morsels. If they don't eat you first...

PLENTY MORE FISH IN THE SEA

For almost as long as they've lived on Earth, people have gone fishing. And in some places, methods haven't changed all that much. Fishermen still use the same trusty old spears, hooks and lines that they've been using for thousands of years. In Papua New Guinea (a country north-east of Australia), fishermen even use giant spiders' webs as nets (though they take the giant spiders out first).

Elsewhere in the world, fishing is big business – around 75 million tonnes of fish are caught every year. (That's a mind-boggling number of fish fingers!) Modern fishing trawlers are horribly high-tech. They find their fish using computers and sonar* and catch them in unbelievably big nets many kilometres long. Some ships are more like floating fish factories. They can clean, pack and freeze the fish while on board. That's bad luck if you happen to be a sardine. You're the fish they catch most of.

* SONAR IS AN INSTRUMENT WHICH SENDS OUT BEEPS OF SOUND. THESE HIT OBJECTS, SUCH AS SARDINES, AND SEND BACK ECHOES. THE ECHOES ARE PICKED UP BY ON-BOARD COMPUTERS AND SHOWN ON A SCREEN, THAT'S HOW YOU TELL WHERE THE FISH ARE.

BEEP! BEEP! FISH

What on Earth are fish?

Of course, you know what fish are but do you know what fish have in common? Any idea which two of these fishy facts are false?

1 Fish are cold-blooded. (Cold-blooded means they have to rely on outside conditions, like water temperature, to warm them up or cool them down.)

2 Fish live in salty and fresh water.

3 Fish breathe oxygen dissolved in the water.

4 Fish breathe through lungs, like humans.

5 Most fish are covered in scales.

6 Fish use their fins for steering and paddling.

7 All fish have bony skeletons.

8 Some fish can live out of water.

Answers: 4 and 7 are false.

4 Fish don't have lungs. Instead they breathe through slitty gills on the sides of their heads. As a fish swims along, it closes its gill covers, opens its mouth and gulps in water. Then it closes its mouth, opens its gills and forces the water out over them. This is when dissolved oxygen from the water goes into the fish's blood.

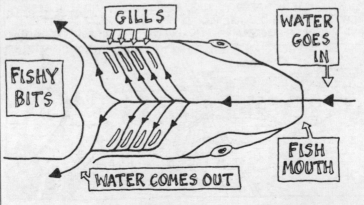

7 Sharks and rays have skeletons made of rubbery cartilage instead of bone. Press the end of your nose with your finger, go on, don't be shy! That's what cartilage feels like.

(By the way number **8** is true, believe it or not. Mudskippers are happy to be fish out of water but they need to keep their skin damp for taking in oxygen. They live at the muddy mouths of some rivers where the river meets the sea.)

Some very fishy record breakers

First The first fish appeared over 500 million years ago. They were just 4 centimetres long...

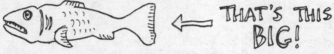

THAT'S THIS BIG!

with tiny teeth. Today, there are 25,000 fascinating fish species. And another hundred are discovered each year. In fact, there are as many different types of fish in the sea as there are amphibians, reptiles, birds and mammals put together. So there!

Fastest There's no catching the sensationally speedy sailfish. Over short distances, it's unbeatable. It races along at over 100 km/h, tucking its fins into its sides, to make it more aerodynamic.

ZOOM!

Slowest Seahorses are not only the oddest-looking fish in the oceans (how on Earth did they get those horse-shaped heads?), they're also the slowest swimmers. A seahorse in a tearing hurry takes three whole days to travel one kilometre! Stranger still, it's dad who has the babies. He grows a small pouch on his belly, into which the female squirts her eggs. (Then she swims off and leaves him to it.) Two weeks later, hundreds of baby seahorses shoot out. The first thing they do is learn to swim upright!

Best fliers To avoid being snapped up by hungry enemies, flying fish shoot out of the sea and glide through the air on wing-like fins. Like tiny fishy aeroplanes. Sometimes their enemies try to follow. A ship's cat was once lost overboard in the Atlantic Ocean, trying to grab a flying fish.

Smallest The titchiest fish in the big blue sea is the tiny dwarf goby from the Indian Ocean. It's so incredibly small it could swim up and down a tablespoon, with plenty of space to spare.

Oldest The longest-lived fish is thought to be an 88-year-old eel, called Putte, who died in 1948. She was born in the Sargasso Sea (part of the Atlantic Ocean) in 1860 but spent most of her life in a Swedish aquarium. Telling the age of a fish isn't easy. First you have to catch your fish and kill it. Then you have to count the growth rings on its scales and bones. Messy!

Greatest size difference In the tough old world of odious oceans, being eaten is a fact of life. So the ocean sunfish lays millions of eggs, to make sure that some survive. The newborn sunfish are the size of peas. But not for long. By the time they're adults, they're over a thousand times bigger – as big and heavy as small trucks. Awesome.

Riskiest to eat If you really want to dice with danger, try a portion of death pufferfish, the deadliest fish in the sea. Despite this, it's eaten as a delicacy in Japan where they call it fugu. Its heart, liver, blood and guts are so horribly poisonous, even the tiniest taste can kill you. Chefs are specially trained to take these bits out. But what if they get it wrong? One slight mistake and you're history.

GET IT RIGHT OR YOU'RE FIRED

First, you'll feel numb all over, then the shakes begin. A cure? Well, there isn't one really, though burying yourself up to your neck in mud is said to help a bit!

Greediest Fish get seasick – it's true! Especially if you shake them about in a bucket! (Don't try this at home!) Or if they eat themselves into a stupor. They don't come much greedier than the bad-mannered bluefish. It eats and eats until it makes itself sick. And then it starts eating all over again! Disgusting.

Largest catch In 1986, a Norwegian fishing boat caught 120 million fish – in one go. That's 30 fish for every Norwegian. The biggest fish ever caught with a rod was a whopping great white shark. It weighed more than a tonne.

And there's plenty more than just fish in the sea...

What on Earth are crabby crustaceans?

Strictly speaking, crustaceans aren't really fish. They're creatures like shrimps, crabs and lobsters. Most of them have hard shells to protect their soft bodies. And most live in water, except for woodlice – you might find one of these under a stone in your garden.

The biggest crustaceans are Japanese spider crabs. They're so huge, you could fit a horse between their huge front claws. They're also called "stilt-crabs" because their legs are so long. The biggest on record had a 3.6-metre legspan, and weighed a massive 18 kilograms. These colossal crustaceans live on the seabed. They eat other crustaceans, worms and molluscs. They won't go for you, though, unless your toes get too close for comfort.

Talking of your toes, you should watch out for the boxer crab. It has one of the nastiest nips. It cheats, though, by holding a stinging sea anemone in each of its pincers. Then, if an enemy gets too close, this crabby crustacean shoves the anemone in its face. Nice! Because its hands are always full, this crackpot crab has to eat with its feet.

At the other end of the size scale are paltry pea crabs. They live inside mussel and oyster shells, picking scraps of food off their gills. Of course, size isn't everything. What krill (small shrimps) lack in size, they easily make up in numbers. They swim about in enormous swarms, weighing up to ten million tonnes. These swarms are so huge they can be spotted by satellites in outer space. They're the staple food of many sea creatures, including fish, seals and mighty blue whales. And they may soon be on the menu for you, too – in Russia, krill is catching on fast. But krill cuisine is trickier than it sounds.

1 First catch some krill. And that's not easy. The biggest swarms live in the freezing Southern Ocean. Byeeee!

2 Process it quickly. Krill goes off very fast. Phwoar!

3 Then give it some flavour. Apart from being vaguely fishy, it doesn't taste of much.

KRILL

4 Last but not least, find something else for blue whales to eat. And make sure there's plenty of it…

If you're looking for a less long-winded lunch, what about lobster? Lobsters are so tasty that people are now their worst enemy! Lobsters are usually brown and speckled but when a chef chucks one into boiling water, it turns bright pink in just six minutes and is cooked and ready to eat. Cruel? Certainly one chef thought so. He tried to hypnotize his lobsters by rubbing their backs before he cooked them, so they wouldn't feel a thing.

Each autumn, thousands of American spiny lobsters trek hundreds of kilometres across the Atlantic seabed. They scurry along in single file, holding on, for safety, to the lobster in front. They travel day and night, up to 60 together, and can cover 50 kilometres without a rest. The aim of their amazing journey is to find fresh supplies of food. They can tell when it's time to get going because of a sharp drop in sea temperature that comes with the first winter storms. It's a long way to go to end up in the pot.

What on Earth are molluscs?

Molluscs aren't fish either. They're creatures like clams, cockles, oysters, squid and octopuses. Like crunchy crustaceans, many molluscs have hard shells to protect their soft, squishy bodies. But not all...

Nine meaty mollusc facts

1 The most massive mollusc is the Atlantic giant squid which can grow a mighty 16 metres long (that's 6 metres of body and 10 metres of terrible tentacles). No wonder it doesn't need a shell as well.

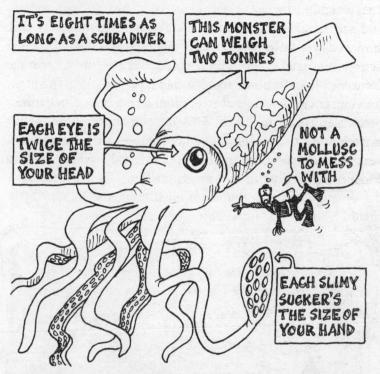

IT'S EIGHT TIMES AS LONG AS A SCUBA DIVER

THIS MONSTER CAN WEIGH TWO TONNES

EACH EYE IS TWICE THE SIZE OF YOUR HEAD

NOT A MOLLUSC TO MESS WITH

EACH SLIMY SUCKER'S THE SIZE OF YOUR HAND

In days gone by, sailors were terrified by tales of a sea monster, large and mean enough to tip up a ship. Its name alone struck fear into their hearts. The blood-curdling kraken. Apparently, it had a mass of sucker-covered tentacles and a sharp, beaky mouth strong enough to bore through the broadest of beams. Sound familiar? Krakens were so big and solid that short-sighted sailors sometimes mistook them for islands and went ashore. One baffled bishop even set up an altar on a kraken's back and knelt down to say his prayers. Ooops! But what was this brutal beast, if it existed? Geographers think it must have been a giant squid, allowing for a bit of exaggeration.

2 In fact, squid are seriously sensitive creatures with nerves 100 times thicker than ours. They're not usually nasty. No way. The only known instance of death by squid was the case of a shipwrecked sailor. A huge squid dragged him screaming from his life-raft, never to be seen again.

3 Odious octopuses are closely related to squid. The largest octopuses live in the Pacific Ocean and measure more than 9 metres across their outstretched tentacles. That's right across your sitting-room. Imagine being hugged by that! Relax. Most octopuses are much, much smaller. The smallest has a 5-cm tentacle-span – that's not much longer than your little finger. A titch by comparison.

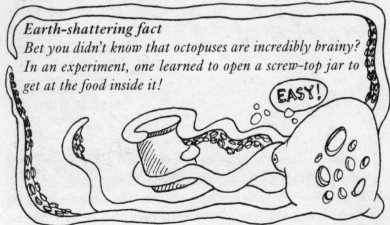

Earth-shattering fact
Bet you didn't know that octopuses are incredibly brainy? In an experiment, one learned to open a screw-top jar to get at the food inside it!

EASY!

4 The cuttlefish is another close cousin. These mild-mannered molluscs wear their shells on the inside, to help them float. You sometimes find them washed up on the

beach. They can also change colour, at the drop of a hat, by making tiny pigment (colour) cells in their skin shrink or grow. This helps them to hide, or attract a mate. If there's no place to hide, they squirt their enemies with thick, black ink while they make their getaway. Cunning.

5 The biggest seashell is the giant clam which hangs around near coral reefs. Some clam shells are so spacious you could hop in and have a nice, long bath. But forget any rumours about your legs getting trapped – the two halves of the shell close much too slowly to do any damage.

6 At high tide, a plough snail sucks water into its tube-shaped foot, then uses it as a surfboard to ride the waves on the lookout for food. When the tide goes out, it heads back to the shore and burrows into the sand.

7 To avoid being swept away with the tide, limpets cling to the rocks with a force 2,000 times their own weight. When the tide goes out, they feed on the green algae which grows on the rocks, moving backwards and forwards across it like tiny lawnmowers.

8 For centuries seashells were used as money. In Africa, you paid 25 cowrie shells for a chicken and 2,500 for a cow. Cowrie shells were also used as jewellery, lucky charms, and even as mummies' eyes. When a king died, in some parts of Asia, nine cowries were stuffed into his mouth for him to use in the next world. Nobles were worth seven cowries; common people just one.

9 And finally, mussels stick to rocks using short, fine, black threads, called their "beards". What's really weird is that the beards are squeezed out of their feet. Weirder still, people in Italy used to collect clumps of mussel beards and weave them into cloth because they felt nice and silky – and probably still do.

Do any of these creatures sound temptingly tasty? Would you know which ones are good enough to eat? Before you get out your knife and fork, try this test on your teacher. We wouldn't want you getting indigestion, now, would we?

Can you eat it?*

The creatures in this quiz are all named after types of food. Because that's what gutsy geographers think they look like. But that doesn't mean to say you can eat them all. Get your teacher to look at this list and say, YUM! for "Yes, I'd eat that," and YUCK! for "No way am I touching that!" (Bear in mind, though, that some people will eat anything…) (*Not suitable for vegetarians or anyone allergic to shellfish. Sorry.)

1: SEA CUCUMBER

2: SEA LEMON

3: PINEAPPLE FISH

4: SEA SPROUT

5: BANANA PRAWN

6: CABBAGE SHRIMP

7: COMB JELLY

8: SEA POTATO

9: SEA TOMATO

10: PEA CRAB

Answers:

1 YUM! The Japanese eat tonnes of the things. Sea cucumbers are small, sausagey creatures, that belong to the starfish and sea urchin family. They roam the seabed, sucking up scraps. If a hungry fish gets too close, they have a dramatic way of defending themselves. They shoot out streams of sticky guts, like strings of spaghetti, which tie the fish up in knots. Then they buzz off. Their guts grow back later, no problem. Fancy a mouthful?

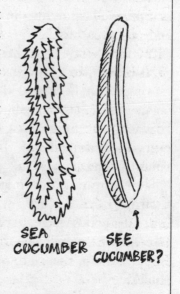

SEA CUCUMBER   SEE CUCUMBER?

2 YUCK! Not recommended. Sea lemons are a type of sea slug (sea snails without seashells). When they're disturbed, they squirt out burning acid. And that's how they get their bitter name.

3 YUM! The pineapple fish looks yellow and spiny, like a pineapple and you can eat it (it's Japan, again!) but don't expect it to taste anything like fruit. On the other hand you could just keep it as a pet. Its odd appearance, combined with the fact that it glows in the dark (it's got two luminous patches under its chin), means you might well spot one in your nearest aquarium.

4 YUCK! Sorry! A red herring.

5 YUM! Most prawns and shrimps can be eaten, though none of them tastes anything like bananas. In South-East Asia, banana prawns (and Indian prawns, tiger prawns and yellow prawns) are raised on huge fish "farms". These are massive saltwater ponds where the prawns are fed on specially nourishing algae to make them grow more quickly.

SEA LEMON

SLICE OF LEMON

PINEAPPLE FISH

PINEAPPLE CHUNKS

BANANA PRAWN

BANANA SKIN

6 YUCK! No such thing. You get clam, cleaner, fairy and mud shrimps. You even get opossum and skeleton shrimps. But you don't get cabbage shrimps.

7 YUCK! Comb jellies look like little glowing globules of jelly, floating through the open sea. But not the sort of jelly you mean. The name "comb" comes from the bristly fringes which the jelly wiggles and waves to propel itself along. Comb jellies don't sting at least, but their sticky tentacles snatch up their supper.

8 YUM! Sea potatoes are really sea urchins, harvested in some parts of the world (with their eggs) for food. Some people eat these with salad. But watch your fingers. Sea urchins are covered in sharp, spiky, often poisonous spines, which protect them from enemies. Including you. Sea potatoes also use their spines for burrowing into the sand to hide.

9 YUCK! There are sea cucumbers and sea lettuces, but no sea tomatoes.

10 YUM! But you'd need an awful lot of them to fill you up.

NICE PLATE OF CABBAGE

COMB JELLY

JELLY WITH COMB

SEA POTATO

MASHED POTATO

PEA CRAB

CRAB PEE

Actually, pea crabs aren't very popular with some fishermen. They live inside edible mussels, spoiling the fisherman's catch.

If nothing so far tickles your tastebuds, how about eating like an Inuit? The Inuit live in the icy Arctic where they fish and hunt seals, walruses and whales, catching them with guns and harpoons. Seals are considered particularly tasty, especially stuffed with little auks (a type of sea bird). They're so important, in fact, that they've become part of Inuit folklore. This ancient Inuit legend explains how the seals came to be in the sea.

How the seals came to live in the sea or A fishy fingered tale

It's never easy being a girl, especially when you've got your dad going on and on at you all of the time. It's even worse when you're the goddess of the sea. Such a lot of responsibility. You never get any time to yourself.

Sedna was the goddess of the sea, and she lived with her father in a house on the shore. She was pretty and witty (and she knew it) and lots of men wanted to marry her. But snooty Sedna turned them all down. Then, one day, a handsome hunter paddled by in his canoe, dressed in splendid furs.

"Follow me," he said to Sedna. "To the land of the birds, where no one goes hungry. Where you'll lie on warm bearskins inside my tent. And your cup will never run dry. Blah! blah! blah!" (Blokes in furs go on a bit.)

How could a girl refuse? Sedna had never seen anyone so handsome in all her life. What was she to do? Her heart said one thing; her head another. The handsome hunter was waiting. Suddenly, she made up her mind and leapt into the canoe, and they paddled off into the sunset together...

Now, the handsome hunter wasn't really a hunter. He was a sea bird spirit disguised as a man. But he'd fallen madly in love with Sedna and wanted to keep her, no matter what. So he kept his mouth (or beak) firmly shut. When Sedna finally found out the truth, she cried and cried for days on end, and wished that she was dead. Then, one day, when the sea bird was out, Sedna's dad turned up at the door. He'd come to take her home again, warm bearskins or no warm bearskins.

When the sea bird returned and looked for his wife, she was nowhere to be seen. Bravely, the wind broke the bad news. And before you could say "Sedna, come home, I may be a simple sea bird but I love you!", he'd changed into a human and hopped into his canoe. He soon caught up with Sedna and her dad. And he begged and begged her to come back home. But her father hid her in the bottom of his little boat and wouldn't let the hunter anywhere near her.

"Right," said the hunter. "I'll show you," he said. What did he do? He turned right back into a sea bird, spread his wings, and, croaking wildly, flapped away to get help from his spirit friends. Suddenly, a terrible storm blew up and swept across the ocean – the spirits were angry on the sea bird's behalf. Somebody would have to pay. Sedna's poor dad was scared to death. He'd feared the spirits all of his life and was hardly likely to stop fearing them now. There was only one thing for it, and he knew it – to make things better, he'd have to sacrifice his precious daughter to the sea. So, he picked her up and … chucked her overboard! Just like that.

Trying desperately to keep her head above water, Sedna gripped the side of the boat as tightly as she could. But her spirit-fearing father would not be put off. He picked up an axe and neatly chopped off her fingers so she couldn't hold on, no way!

Slowly but surely, Sedna sank beneath the waves but, amazingly, her fingers survived. And they turned into the seals, whales and walruses which live in the sea today. Then the storm died down and the sea grew calm and the spirits were contented. Sedna's dad made his sad way home, trying to put the whole thing behind him. But later that night, the highest tide ever seen covered the shore and swallowed him up, house and all, and carried him down to the depths of the sea. There he met his daughter again. What she said when she saw him is anybody's guess.

Now, if the Inuit want to make sure that they have plenty of seals and walruses to catch, one of them goes into a deep, deep trance. In his mind's eye, he travels down to the bottom of the sea to ask Sedna to send them good hunting. And sometimes she does, and sometimes she doesn't.

OIL AND OTHER OCEAN SPOILS

Now, forget for a moment about fish, crabs, molluscs and seals. There's other stuff down under that you could put to good use. From salt to seaweed, sunken treasure to shipwrecks, pearls to precious metals, the sea is full of valuables. Some are horribly hard to find. Take gold, for example. There's masses of gold hanging around in sea water – about seven million tonnes in total. That's enough for everyone in the world to have a good, big chunk each. But getting it out is another story. Other things are easier to extract. Oil is one of the great ocean spoils…

1 One-fifth of all the oil we use comes from under the sea. Here's how it got there, and how we found it:
a) Millions of years ago, the sea was full of tiny plants and animals.

b) When they died, their bodies sank to the seabed.

c) They were buried under layers of sand and mud.

d) The sand and mud turned into rock …

e) … and squashed the bodies into thick, gungy oil.

f) This seeped upwards until it was trapped by harder rock above.

g) Millions of years passed. Then along came some geologists – scientists whose job is to study rocks. Geologists can guess where oil lies by looking carefully at the structure of the rocks on the seabed. Clever.

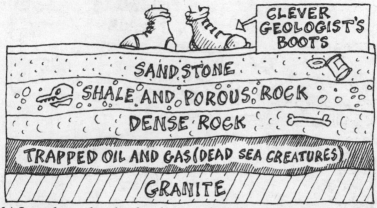

h) In order to be absolutely sure there is oil they have to drill a test hole. If they strike lucky, they're away, and can build a proper oil rig, with a pipeline that pumps the oil to a refinery on land. Supplies are brought on board and there's plenty of work for plenty of people.

i) An unlucky strike means going back to stage **g)** and trying again … and again, and again. Not so clever.

The world's main offshore oil fields are in the Middle East, the USA, Central and South America and the North Sea. Oil was first found under the North Sea in the 1960s. And what a fabulous find! A staggering 3.2 million barrels of oil are pumped out of the North Sea each day, and it's worth millions and millions of pounds. A single rig pumps up enough oil in a day to fill 70,000 cars with petrol.

2 Great as it seems, the oil isn't going to last for ever. And stocks are starting to run low. So what can we do? Well, there are other ways of finding energy from the sea. One idea is to collect the power of the tides and turn it into electricity. There's also Ocean Thermal Energy Conversion – that's a bit of a mouthful, so you can call it OTEC for short. The idea here is that scientists can use the difference in temperature between warm water on the surface of the sea and colder water deeper down to make electricity. In fact, OTEC sites are already working well in Hawaii, Japan, Florida and Cuba.

3

SEAWEED
IT'S THE GREEN STUFF THAT'S GOOD FOR YOU

1. FERTILIZE YOUR FIELDS WITH IT. SPREAD IT ON NICE AND THICK, IT'S A GREAT ALTERNATIVE TO PONGY HORSE POO... ...THOUGH IT PONGS MUCH THE SAME!

2. COOK IT! IT'S FULL OF HEALTHY VITAMINS AND MINERALS, TRY IT LIGHTLY FRIED WITH AN EGG ON TOP!

3. BRUSH YOUR TEETH WITH IT! ITS SECRET INGREDIENT IS A GOO CALLED CARRAGEENAN, WHICH MAKES TOOTHPASTE THICKER

4. BLOW THINGS UP! YES, SEAWEED CONTAINS A SUBSTANCE USED IN BOMBS!

5. DRINK IT... ...IF YOU'RE OVER 18, IT'S AN INGREDIENT IN BEER.

6. AND IF YOU'RE A SEA OTTER, IT MAKES A PERFECT ANCHOR TO STOP YOU DRIFTING OUT TO SEA, AS YOU DRIFT OFF TO SLEEP, ZZZZ!

65

4 Why not season your seaweed with a pinch of sea salt? We eat six million tonnes of the stuff a year. In hot countries, collecting salt is easy. You dig a big, shallow pool along the coast and call it a salt pan. Then wait around for the tide to come in. The sea fills the pans, then the water evaporates (dries up) in the sun, and you're left with a layer of salt. Simple!

5 Taking the salt out of seawater can be useful in other ways too. In hot, dry desert countries such as those around the Persian Gulf in the Middle East, there are huge desalination plants (that's factory-type plants, not the green, leafy variety) along the coast. Here salt is extracted, leaving clean, fresh water for drinking. Brilliant.

Earth-shattering fact
Did you know that the finest fertilizer isn't seaweed, or horse poo, or even mouldy old teabags around your roses (honestly!). It's unsavoury seabird poo! Cormorant droppings, or ghastly guano (gwaano), are 50 times more fertile than horse poo. And smellier! So many cormorants once nested along the coast of Peru that the guano was deep enough to bury a house. Phew!

6 For deep-sea spoils, dive to the bottom of the great Pacific Ocean. It's covered in billions of dirty black lumps. They're called manganese nodules (nodule is a posh word for lump, that's all). Inside one of these nautical nodules you'll also find iron, nickel and copper. They've got a weird way of growing: over millions of years, layers of metal stick to a shark's tooth or a clump of sand, and that's it. They can be as small as a golfball to the size of a football. So all you have to do is collect them up and make your fortune. The big question is, how? Scientists are hoping that a machine which works a bit like a gigantic vacuum cleaner, and is carried by ship, will do the trick.

Pearls, pearls, pearls

If you really want to spoil yourself, treat yourself to a string of pearls. Pearls are one of the most precious ocean spoils. First, you'll have to find an irritable oyster. Why? Well, oysters, clams and mussels sometimes get pesky parasites inside their shells. You know when you've got an itch right in the middle of your back, always just out of reach? That's how annoying it can be. What do you think they do?

a) Rub up against a sea urchin's spines?

b) Smother it with mother-of-pearl?

c) Ignore it and hope it goes away?

The answer is b). The oyster tries the smother the itch with mother-of-pearl, or nacre (naker), the shiny stuff that lines its shell. And it works like a dream. But there's more. It can take years, true, but eventually, little by little, the nacre builds up into a gleaming, round pearl.

Pearls are not always pearly white. Far from it. They can be pink, purple, green, grey, or even black. And they come in a wide range of sizes. The biggest pearl ever came from a huge giant clam. It was the size of a watermelon, but brain shaped! And it had a strange story to go with it.

Legend says that the pearl started life some 2,500 years ago, when a Chinese philosopher, Lao-Tzu, placed a small lucky charm inside a clam shell. Don't ask me why.

Inside the clam, the pearl started to grow.

Sometime in the 1500s, pearl and shell were caught in a typhoon and lost ... until a deep-sea diver found them again 400 years later.

The pearl was given to a Muslim chief who sold it to an American archaeologist. It recently went on sale again, for the earth-shattering sum of ... £20 million!

People who gaze into the pearl are said to see the faces of the Buddha, Confucius (another Chinese philosopher) and old Lao-Tzu himself.

Today, pearls are very big business. The bigger, rounder, shinier … and pinker (that's the costliest colour), the better. But natural pearls are horribly expensive, because it's so tricky getting them out of the sea. Pearl-divers of old risked their lives every time they went to work. Their equipment was horribly basic – a nose clip, a basket and a weighted rope for lowering them to the seabed. They didn't have tanks of air to breathe – they just dived until they ran out of breath. Perilous! Prising open a clam and spying a pearl inside must be a magical moment. But is it worth risking your life for? Hardly. It wasn't the divers who made all the money – they got peanuts for their pearls.

As demand for pearls grew, the son of a Japanese noodle-seller had a brilliant idea. No more lives need be put in danger. He invented "cultured" pearls. No, it didn't mean they'd read more books or had better table manners than ordinary pearls. What happens is this:

1 An official oyster-irritator opens an oyster…

2 …and slips a slither of shell (usually mussel) inside.

3 Then he closes the shell, puts it back in the sea and waits.

4 The shell smothers the itch with nacre, then…

5 …three years later, the shell is opened, and, hey presto!, inside is a beautiful pearl.

Some far-fetched facts about oysters and pearls

1 Is your pearl real or fake? Try this test. Gently rub the pearl along the front of your teeth. It'll feel gritty if it's natural or cultured. If it's smooth, bad luck. It's a fake.

2 Powdered pearl was once used in love potions (and in cures for madness). Other people think that eating oysters makes you…

a) taller?

b) brainier?

c) sick?

3 Pearl-divers in the Pacific had an ingenious way of taming sharks. To give themselves time to collect the pearls, they sent the sharks into a trance by … "kissing" them on the nose. Not a problem with a nerdy old nurse shark. But kissing a tiger shark could be your last big adventure!

4 Oysters sometimes grow on trees. Honestly. That's because baby oysters like something to cling to, so branches are lowered into the water to give them a perch. After two or three months, the branches are brought up and the oysters bunged into barrels which are sunk back into the sea. Then you still have a long wait before the pearls are finally ready.

5 Dirty water can cause havoc with poor old oysters. In Japan, oysters have to have a good, regular wash to keep them pearly clean.

6 Not every oyster makes a pearl. That's what makes it so exciting…

Terrors of the high seas

At least oyster farmers make an honest living. Which is more than can be said of pirates of old. Their idea of ocean spoils was boarding a passing merchant ship, tying up or gruesomely killing the crew, and making off with as much lovely loot as they could carry. They were mad, bad and dangerous to know. But they didn't care. They wanted gold and they wanted it NOW.

Teacher teaser

Would your teacher make a good pirate? Ask her this cunning question as a test.

Answer: Because they believed it improved their eyesight!
Why does your teacher wear gold earrings?

The terrible tale of Bonny and Read or Anything boys can do, girls can do better!

Of all the perilous pirates who roamed the high seas, two of the ghastliest were girls. Anne Bonny and Mary Read. They were awful enough apart. Together, they were deadly. This is the story of their hair-raising lives, and their sticky ends…

In those days, women were banned from pirate ships. If they were found on board, they were killed, along with anyone who had helped them. The only way for women to become pirates was to disguise themselves as men. And this is exactly what our horrible heroines did.

Mary Read was born in Plymouth, England, in 1690 and spent most of her girlhood dressed as a boy. Why? Well, Mary's granny had pots of cash and Mary's mother wanted a share of it. So she tricked poor old granny into leaving her money to Mary. But she had to pretend that Mary was a rosy-cheeked boy because granny *hated* girls!

By the age of 14, Mary had had enough. She left home

and ran away to sea. Still dressed as a man, she fought in the army at Flanders, Belgium, then fell in love with a handsome soldier (he'd seen through her disguise). Did they live happily ever after? No, they didn't. The handsome soldier fell ill and died, leaving Mary with a broken heart. Sadly, she took to sea once more in a merchant ship, bound for the calming Caribbean Sea.

Meanwhile ... Anne Bonny's life was taking just as strange a turn as Mary's. Her dad was a wealthy Irish lawyer but settling down, like a well-brought up girl should, wasn't Anne's style. By the age of 16, she had a taste for adventure. She ran off and married a sailor who was handsome but weak and the pair hitched a lift on a pirate ship which was also bound for the Caribbean. As soon as she clapped eyes on him, Anne fell in love with the ship's dashing captain, "Calico" Jack Rackham.

He got his nickname from his stripy, calico trousers – his absolute pride and joy. He was cruel, ruthless (quite possibly bearded) and ... utterly irresistible! Anne ditched the sailor, donned cabin boy's clothes and joined dashing Calico Jack and his crew. (Calico knew Anne was a girl but he wasn't going to let on.)

One day, a fine merchant ship came sailing towards them. "Board!" growled Calico Jack. He was a man of few words.

The pirates captured the ship and forced a Dutch sailor, young Mark Reid, to join their band. Soon Anne grew tired of Calico Jack (and his terrible trousers) and fell in love with mysterious Mark. Who didn't seem interested, for some strange reason.

It wasn't long before the truth came out – Mark was Mary, and Anne was not really a cabin boy. With their secret safe, the two joined forces and became the most famous double act since South China and Sea. They were by far the fiercest fighters in Calico's crew, and by far the best at cursing and swearing. In fact, their meanness put the men to shame. In 1720, when the ship was finally captured, only Mary and Anne stayed on deck to fight. The rest of the crew, who were rolling drunk (including clapped-out Calico), ran away and hid below deck.

This time, though, their luck was out. They were captured and tried for piracy, found guilty and sentenced to death. Calico Jack and his men were hanged. On the night before he went to the gallows, Anne visited him in his cell.

"If you'd fought like a man," she shouted, "you'd not be about to hang like a dog!" That told him.

Anne and Mary were spared the execution because both were expecting babies.

"My lord, we plead our bellies," they said in their defence.

They had a lucky escape. But Mary died later in prison. Anne survived, but vanished without trace, though it probably wasn't very long before she'd fallen in love all over again.

Piracy by the rules

By being women, Anne and Mary were breaking one of the first rules of piracy. And there were plenty of pirate rules. Pirates swore them on a Bible (or an axe) before setting out on a voyage. Would you have been able to stick to the rules?

1 You will have an equal say in the ship's running and an equal share of food and strong drink (except in emergencies).

2 You will get a fair share of the spoils. But if you steal from the ship, you'll be marooned (being left on your own in the middle of nowhere). If you steal from another man, you'll have your ears and nose cut off and be thrown overboard.

3 Gambling for money is strictly forbidden.

4 All lights and candles must be out by eight o'clock. If you want to stay up drinking, you can sit on deck in the dark.

5 You must keep your sword, cutlass and pistols clean, primed and ready for action.

6 Women are absolutely banned on board. Under no circumstances whatsoever. On pain of death.

7 The punishment for abandoning ship in battle is death or marooning.

8 Fighting on board is strictly forbidden. Any quarrels will be settled on shore by pistol or sword, as follows…

a) Stand back to back.

b) When the quartermaster gives the word, turn and fire.

c) If you both miss the target (i.e. each other), go back to stage **a)** and try again with your cutlasses (swords).

d) The first to draw blood is the winner.

9 You cannot leave the ship until your share's worth £1,000. (Note: You could bump up your pay by getting injured. Anyone who lost a limb in the course of duty got 800 pieces of eight. The going rate for losing an eye was 100 pieces of eight.)

10 It pays to get promoted. The captain and quartermaster receive double shares. The master gunner and boatswain one and a half shares; officers one and a quarter, and everyone else one each.

Perilous pirates today

You're probably thinking, phew, it's a good job all that stuff's ancient history! Well, sadly, that's where you're wrong... All the following pirate attacks happened in the last ten years. In fact, about 150 attacks are reported each year, especially in the perilous seas around Asia, Africa and South America. But the real total may be twice that number, and growing all the time. Today's pirates are in it for money, valuables and other goods to sell. And they don't care how they get it. The situation has got so serious that the International Maritime Bureau (IMB) set up a centre in Malaysia for monitoring pirates and their activities. It relies on information from ex-members of pirate gangs which is then passed on to shipping companies to warn them to protect their cargoes. It's a horribly risky business all round. And the details must be kept top secret.

PIRATE ATTACKS - TOP SECRET FILES

DATE OF ATTACK: December 1992

LOCATION: Java Sea, off Indonesia (Pacific Ocean)

SHIP: Baltimar Zephir

DETAILS OF ATTACK: Armed pirates board the ship at night, they take over the ship as the crew tries to hide. The British captain's SOS call is ignored by the passing ships who claim it is too dangerous to sail to his rescue. The pirates shoot the captain and first mate dead, steal the crew's valuables and make off in a small speed boat. They are never caught.

DATE OF ATTACK: January 1993

LOCATION: South China Sea (Pacific Ocean)

SHIP: East Wood

DETAILS OF ATTACK: The ship, en route from Hong Kong to Taiwan, is seized by 30 machete-wielding pirates, and the captain is ordered to sail towards Hawaii. The 500 chinese passengers are persuaded to pay the pirates £10,000 each, in return for visas to enter the USA, and the chance of a better life. Neither of which they get.

The plan is foiled after the radio officer manages to alert the US coastguard

DATE OF ATTACK: August 1992

LOCATION: Luzon strait, north of the Philippines (Pacific Ocean)

SHIP: World Bridge

DETAILS OF ATTACK: A gang of 15 pirates, claiming to be members of the chinese navy, open fire at the ship with machine guns and order the captain to stop. When he refuses, they reopen fire and hurl fire crackers on to the deck.

Incredibly, the ship survives, with 50 bullet holes in its side. It is carrying a cargo of highly explosive gas, oil and kerosene!

DANGER EXPLOSIVE

78

DATE OF ATTACK: August 1991

LOCATION: Malaysian Coast (Pacific Ocean)

SHIP: Springstar

DETAILS OF ATTACK: 25 Pirates armed with automatic rifles, hijack the ship, shoot dead the chief officer and dump his body overboard. They lock the crew in their quarters for two days, and make off with Springstar's cargo – £1·5 million worth of electronic goods.

These are later sold illegally in Singapore.

DATE OF ATTACK: September 1995

LOCATION: Gulf of Thailand (Pacific Ocean)

SHIP: Anna Sierra

DETAILS OF ATTACK: The ship is sailing from Bangkok to Manila with a cargo of sugar worth £2·7 million. Just after midnight, it is hijacked by 30 armed, masked men. The terrified crew are put into dinghies and set adrift without supplies. (They are later rescued by Vietnamese fishermen.) The pirates repaint the ship and rename it Arctic Sea, then they sail it to China where they sell the stolen sugar. By September the ship has been tracked down and the pirate crew captured.

True, some pirates do get away with it. But not all of them. Modern-day pirates have to be careful. One was caught out when he left his mobile phone behind on the ship he'd just robbed. The police made a few calls and managed to track him and his gang down.

Of course, none of these deeds of derring-do, ancient or modern, would have been possible without … ships. So, all aboard, me hearties, for the next leg of your horrible voyage.

OCEAN LOCOMOTION

Ships. Where on Earth would we be without them? Sitting at home, high and dry, maybe? For centuries, people have messed about in boats, gone fishing in them, explored the world in them, set off on daring voyages of trade and discovery, even pillaged, plundered and conquered in them. Without ships and boats, Columbus would never have discovered America. No one would ever have made a film about the *Titanic*. And you'd never have tasted a bag of crisps. (Potatoes were brought over from South America in the 16th century. By ship.) Ships started off as simple canoes which were handy for crossing streams and things. Since then, they've got bigger, better and sturdier for travelling much, much further afield. Here are just some of the ships that have made history.

Ships that made a splash!

7,000 BC(ish)   The first boat is made from a pine log (not to be confused with a ship's log) in Holland. Some horrible geographers say it isn't a ship at all. What do they think it is?

How to make a dug-out canoe

You will need:
a tree trunk (the straighter the better)
an axe
some planks
lots of patience

What to do:
1 Chop the tree down (ask permission first).

2 Hollow out the middle with your axe.

3 Turn it upside down and hold it over a fire. This will open it up so you can sit in it. (You might need help with this bit.)

4 Put a couple of planks inside for seats.

5 Start paddling!

3,000 BC   The ancient Egyptians invent sails. They are made from reeds and are square (the sails, that is, not the ancient Egyptians).

2,300 BC   The ancient Egyptians invent the navy too. They send it on a couple of expeditions to conquer new lands and do a bit of trade in luxury goods like cedar wood.

*c.*333 BC	Alexander the Great explores the depths of the Aegean Sea in a glass barrel. So we're told.
AD 800	The Vikings build longships. These are long, narrow warships which are super-fast for launching surprise attacks, and super-light for carrying up rivers. This means the vile Vikings can terrorize more places than ever. To scare their enemies, the ships are given nasty names like *Long Serpent* or *Black Raven of the Wind*. And have fierce-looking dragons carved on the front of them.

900	The Chinese invent ships with several sails instead of one which makes them go much faster. They also invent rudders for steering.

1400	Three-masted ships are built in Europe. With even more sails, they can go even further and even faster.

1620	Cornelius van Drebbel of Holland builds the first submarine. Basically, it's a wooden barrel

covered in leather. He rows it up the River Thames in London, underwater.

1783   A French nobleman, the Marquis Jouffroy d'Abbans, invents the steamboat. For the next 100 years, steam power rules the waves.

1820s   Clipper ships are built in America to carry tea and wool. They get their name because they "clip" so much time off journeys.

1885   The first oil tanker is launched. Today's supertankers are the biggest ships afloat. A ULCC (Ultra Large Crude Carrier) can carry 500,000 tonnes of oil.

Earth-shattering fact
In February 1996, a smallish oil tanker (by oil tanker standards) called Sea Empress, ran aground off the coast of Wales and leaked a lethal 72,500 tonnes of oil. It smothered 1,300 sq km of sea in filthy goo, coated 200 kilometres of coastline and killed thousands of birds, fish and seals. Cleaning up the mess will take years and years.

1955 The world's first nuclear-powered submarine, USS *Nautilus*, is built in the USA. In its first two years, it travels 99,800 kilometres without having to stop and refuel. In 1958, it becomes the first ship to reach the North Pole (by sailing there under the ice).

1955 British inventor, Christopher Cockerell invents the hovercraft. He stumbles across the idea one day, while messing about with a coffee tin, some cat food, a bit of a hoover and some scales. Honestly!

1960s The first ROVs (unmanned Remote-Operated Vehicles) are launched. They are used for exploring the best bits of the deep sea.

1990 SeaCat, the world's biggest catamaran, a boat with two hulls, is launched in Britain. (A hull is the nautical name for a ship's body.) It is twice as fast as a passenger ferry.

With all those ships sailing back and forth, there's bound to be the odd collision. In fact, the Straits of Dover in the English Channel are so overcrowded, the ships have to stay in lanes, like cars on a motorway. But no matter how carefully boats are designed and journeys are planned, accidents will happen. Here's one you've probably heard about before...

That sinking feeling – the terrible tale of RMS Titanic
Going back in time a bit...

On the evening of 14 April 1912, all was quiet on RMS *Titanic*, the biggest, most luxurious liner ever built. She was on the fourth day of her maiden voyage from Southampton to New York, sailing across the North Atlantic, with 2,201 people on board. One of the passengers asked about safety.

MADAM, GOD HIMSELF COULD NOT SINK THIS SHIP!

No one had any reason to doubt him. The *Titanic* was built of the finest steel, with no expense spared. She was 260 metres long and nine decks high, taller than a ten-storey building. She had four huge funnels, each wide enough to drive a train through, and three huge anchors, weighing as much as eight cars each. There had never been a finer ship.

At midday on Wednesday 10 April 1912, the *Titanic* slid majestically out of Southampton harbour. A brass band played and cheering crowds lined the quayside to wave the ship off. Her passengers, among them some of the world's richest people, settled down to enjoy themselves – the ship had its own swimming-pool, tennis courts, palm garden, Turkish baths, billiard hall, dark room for amateur photographers: you name it, it had it. The *Titanic* had everything. For four blissful days, things couldn't have looked easier.

Then, suddenly, on Sunday 14 April, things started to go horribly wrong...

Sunday, 14 April

During the day, the weather gets worse and the *Titanic* receives seven ice warnings from other ships.

11.40 pm The lookouts report an iceberg dead ahead. The ship swings hard to port (left) to avoid it. But it moves too late. The iceberg scrapes the ship's starboard (right) side, gashing a hole in the hull. On the upper decks (first class), all that the passengers notice is a grinding noise and a slight jolt. Many of them don't even wake up. On the lower decks, it's a different story...

11.50 pm Water pours into the front of the ship, and keeps rising.

The ship is brought slowly to a juddering halt.

Monday, 15 April

12.00 am The extent of the damage now becomes clear – unbelievably, the ship is sinking. A distress signal is sent out on the radio. The captain orders the lifeboats to be uncovered. But it turns out that the *Titanic* only has enough lifeboats for half its passengers and crew.

12.25 am The situation gets worse. Orders are given to load women and children into the lifeboats first. The men are left on deck, waving goodbye to their loved ones. Some women refuse to leave their husbands. Hopes are raised when a ship's lights come into view. But the ship turns and steams away again. It doesn't even seem to have seen them.

12.35 am Two other ships, the *Carpathia* and the *Mount Temple*, about 80 kilometres away, pick up the *Titanic*'s SOS and head towards her at full speed.

12.45 am The first lifeboat is lowered, less than half full. And the first of eight distress flares are fired.

1.00–2.00 am More lifeboats leave. The ship is now tilting steeply. Hundreds of people remain on board. The ship's band strikes up a cheery tune to keep their spirits up.

2.17 am The captain gives the order to abandon ship.
2.18 am The ship's lights blink once, then go out for good.

Two minutes later, at 2.20 am, the *Titanic* turned on her end and sank

At 4.00 am, the *Carpathia* finally reached the terrible scene and rescued more than 700 people from the lifeboats. But many passengers died floating in their lifejackets in the icy sea. A total of 1,490 lives were lost.

Some risky reasons why the Titanic sank

1 She hit an iceberg. In April, in the North Atlantic, icebergs and pack ice are common hazards for ships. The iceberg that sank the *Titanic* was small and dark, and seven-eighths lay hidden underwater. By the time the lookouts spotted it, it was already much too late.

2 Despite seven ice warnings, the *Titanic* was travelling at full steam ahead. Far too fast for such icy seas.

3 The ship was declared watertight by its builders. It had a double-layered bottom and 15 watertight compartments making up the area below decks. The idea was that, if even three or four flooded, the *Titanic* would still be able to float. As it happened, water poured into the first five compartments, then spilled over into the others. The ship was doomed.

4 Did the collision trigger a massive explosion in the ship's coal bunker, (The *Titanic* was a steam ship, powered by coal.) blowing a hole in the side? Some experts think so. Strangely, the ship had set sail from Southampton with one of its bunkers on fire.

5 Stranger still, some people blamed an Egyptian mummy being shipped across to America. Nicknamed "Shipwrecker", it was said to be cursed. Rumour had it that, just as the captain gave the order to abandon ship, the mummy appeared on deck. Spooky.

Earth-shattering fact
There are lots of superstitions that some people believe can cause a ship to sink. For example, you should never launch a ship on a Friday. It's said to be the unluckiest day of the week because it was the day on which Jesus Christ was crucified. In the 19th century, the British navy decided to end this nonsense once and for all. They launched a ship called HMS Friday, on a Friday, with a Captain Friday in command. Guess what? It sank without trace!

WHY COULDN'T WE HAVE HAD CAPTAIN WEDNESDAY?

Whatever the reason for the *Titanic* tragedy, going to sea would never be the same again. It was safety first from now on. By law, ships had to carry enough lifeboats for everyone on board. Emergency and safety drills were improved. And lookouts had to have regular eye tests. And the watertight bulkheads now had to extend upwards right to the weather deck. In the North Atlantic, the International Ice Patrol was set up to warn ships of hazards. And no one ever claimed that a ship was unsinkable ever again. They didn't dare.

Is a sailor's life for you?

But what about the people who had to sail all these ships? You might think your life is horrible, what with too much homework and too little pocket money. But is it really bad enough to make you run away to sea? Count your lucky stars you weren't a sailor in days gone by. Here's an example of what you might have had for your supper.

On the mouldy menu today…

MAIN COURSE: &
LOBSCOUSE
ROPE-YARNS OR BABIES' HEADS
SERVED WITH
TRAIN SMASH & GALLY PEPPER

DESSERT: &
FIGGY-DUFF
OR
DANDY-FUNK

Roughly translated, that's…

MAIN COURSE:
RAISIN BISCUIT AND SALT-MEAT STEW
TINNED MEAT OR CANNED MEAT PUDDING
SERVED WITH:
TINNED TOMATOES AND SMUTS (SMUTS WERE ASHES
FROM THE FIRE THAT FELL INTO THE COOKING POTS.
NOBODY BOTHERED TO PICK THEM OUT AGAIN.)

DESSERT:
RAISIN PUDDING
OR
BROKEN BISCUIT PIE (WITH THE ODD WEEVIL - THAT'S
A SMALL CREEPY CRAWLY THROWN IN FOR FLAVOUR.)

Rum rations
No wonder sailors looked forward to their daily ration of
grog (rum and water). They needed it to wash their Babies'
Heads down!

Sick as a sea dog

If the food didn't get you first, the seasickness might. Even the saltiest old sea dogs got seasick. Including Horatio Lord Nelson, Britain's best-known sailor. On his very first voyage, he was horribly seasick for months on end. And 30 years later, he was still being sick. (He also suffered from yellow fever, scurvy, malaria and bouts of depression, but that's another story…) It's the rocking motion of the boat that's the problem. It upsets your balance and confuses your brain. Which makes you feel sick. Is there a cure? Well, sort of. Many cures have been tried and failed. Staring straight ahead at the horizon can help. Or you can wear a seasickness wristband. The plastic button on the strap presses against a sensitive spot on your wrist and makes you feel better. At least, that's the theory… Most cures, unfortunately, just send you to sleep. Zzzzzzzz!

A British inventor, Sir Henry Bessemer, had a brilliant idea for beating seasickness on cross-channel steamships. He devised a "swinging saloon" which balanced on a central pivot and was meant to stay on an even keel, no matter how much the ship rocked and rolled. Sir Henry, who was always seasick himself, hoped to put a stop to it once and for all. Unfortunately, the saloon swung so violently that some people were seasick who'd never been seasick before!

93

Dreadful food and seasickness sound bad enough? Worse things can happen to a sailor...

Adrift on a raft

Imagine being all alone at sea. With only a seagull for company. You'd soon get hopelessly lonely and bored. The first week would be bad enough. But what on Earth would you do by week ten? Or 19? Someone who knew just how this felt was a young sailor, called Poon Lim, who proved one of the sea's greatest survivors. This is his real-life story...

On 23 November 1942, the SS *Ben Lomond*, a ship in the British Merchant Navy, was torpedoed by a German submarine in the Atlantic, some 565 miles west of Britain. It was the Second World War. Poon Lim was 25, he was the second steward on the ship – and he was the only one who survived the attack. His day had started off badly, and soon got worse. Before his ship sank, Poon Lim realized he needed to act, and fast. He grabbed a life-raft and some supplies and clambered on board. He had enough food and water for 50 days. Never in his wildest dreams did poor Poon Lim imagine he'd be on board for more than a day or two.

94

But 50 days later, there he was. When his food ran out, Poon Lim had to live by his wits. He took the metal spring out of his pocket torch and shaped it into a fish-hook.

Then he ground up some biscuit crumbs into paste for bait and started fishing. Unfortunately, fish was all there was. For almost three months, Poon Lim lived on a diet of raw fish (and the odd slither of seagull), washed down with handfuls of rainwater.

Several times, Poon Lim was almost rescued. Almost, but not quite. Finally, on 5 April 1943, he was picked up by a fishing boat off the coast of Brazil. He'd spent a total of 133 days alone on his raft, a record that has never been broken. Amazingly, after all he'd been through, he only had a bit of tummy ache. Apart from that, he was fit and well. He was awarded the British Empire Medal for his incredible courage.

But when, some time later, Poon Lim applied to join the US Navy, he was turned down. Why do you think that was?

a) Because he couldn't swim.

b) Because he got seasick.

c) Because he had flat feet.

Do you have what it takes to join the Navy?

Fancy a life on the ocean waves? The good news is that the Navy today isn't quite as harsh as it used to be (although some sailors might say that the food is just as bad). The bad news is that to get in, you have to pass some nasty nautical tests…

Stage 1: Have you got what it takes?

Answer the following questions – it's best to be honest! Are you:

a) Over 18? (If you're only 12, you'll have to wait. If you're 16 or 17, you'll need your parents' permission.)

b) Physically fit? (You'll soon be even fitter.)

c) Keen to learn? (If you're running away to the Navy to escape from school, forget it. You'll be kicking off your new career with eight weeks of hard training.)

d) Well educated? (Errr, if you're not sure, ask a teacher.)

e) Able to swim? (For obvious reasons!)

COULD I HAVE A WORD, PETERSON?

f) Good at ironing? (You'll have to learn fast. Your kit has to be kept in tip-top condition for inspection.)

g) Good at teamwork? (You'll be spending a lot of time with the same bunch of people – and that's not just in the daytime, you'll be sleeping in the same room as well.)

If you answered yes to most of these questions, go on to the next stage. If you've more nos than yeses, OK, you're excused, you can skip to the end of the chapter.

Stage 2: Have you got any brains?
See how naturally nautical you are by answering these real Navy entrance questions. But be quick. You've only got 15 seconds to answer question 1 and 2 and 30 seconds for question 3. On your marks, get set, go!

① WORD IS TO PAGE AS CHAPTER IS TO...

a) LINE   b) VERSE   c) READING

d) BOOK   e) SECTION

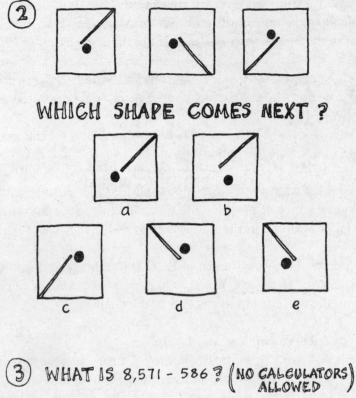

WHICH SHAPE COMES NEXT ?

②

a

b

c

d

e

③ WHAT IS 8,571 - 586 ? (NO CALCULATORS ALLOWED)

A) 7,995   B) 8,015

C) 7,985   D) 8,085   E) 7,085

If you got two or more right, go on to the next stage. One or less, you can skip to the end of the chapter.

Stage 3: Have you got any muscles?

OK, so you don't have to be Mr or Miss Universe, but if you're the sort of person who'll do anything to get out of PE, you're heading for the wrong career. Parading, working out in the gym, cross-country running and assault courses are just a few of the exhausting exercises you'll be expected to enjoy.

You'll need a thorough medical examination, too. And you can fail if you suffer from:

But it all depends on what job you want to do (see below). For example, good eyesight is crucial for a pilot. Stands to reason.

Are you fighting fit? Then congratulations! You've passed! On with your eight weeks of training. It's a bit different from school, though. Your timetable's going to include learning how to tie ropes up in knots (or bends and hitches, as they're called at sea); how to march properly (and that's not as simple as it looks); how to keep your kit clean (no, you can't take your mum with you).

If you get through all this, you're ready for "trade" training which teaches you how to do a particular job. Here are a few you could choose from:

NOTICE BOARD

DIVER

WEAPONS INSTRUCTOR

NURSE

TRANSLATOR

MECHANIC

SURVEYOR

SUB-CREW

CHEF OR SHIP'S STEWARD

WRITER

ENGINEER

ACCOUNTANT

REWARD
HAS ANYONE SEEN THIS FISH?

DRUMMER OR BUGLER

PILOT

It can take a few weeks, or it can take years, but once you're through training, you're ready for action! Ah … didn't you realize, being in the Navy means if there's a war on, you'll probably be in the thick of things. Still want to join…?

What if you're happy being a land-loving lazybones, get terrible seasickness or are just plain scared? Well, you're in good company, there are plenty of us who don't fancy a life at sea. Maybe you'd rather read about adventure and excitement instead? Well, brace yourself. You're about to meet some of the greatest explorers in the whole history of the salty seas.

ODIOUS EXPLORATION

For thousands of years, intrepid explorers have sailed the seas in search of adventure. Some had specific adventures in mind, like discovering new lands or new places to trade. Others didn't know where they were going. They simply set off as the fancy took them.

The plucky Polynesians

The plucky Polynesians were exploring the vast Pacific Ocean over 2,000 years ago. Long before anyone else had heard of it. They loaded their huge dug-out canoes with people, plants and animals, and set off to find new islands to live on. Including New Zealand. And Easter Island. And Hawaii, to name but a few. They were born sailors, the Polynesians. And incredibly ingenious. They had to be. They didn't have charts, compasses, telescopes or any other mod cons to help them navigate. Instead they followed the sun, stars, clouds, and mysterious bundles of … sticks! Actually these stick maps were unbelievably useful. They were used for teaching budding sailors to find islands without actually seeing them. Even from 150 kilometres away.

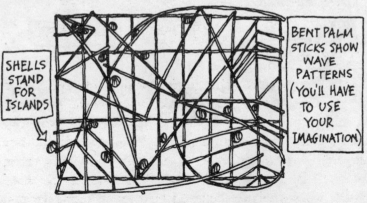

SHELLS STAND FOR ISLANDS

BENT PALM STICKS SHOW WAVE PATTERNS (YOU'LL HAVE TO USE YOUR IMAGINATION)

The intrepid Egyptians

In about 600 BC, Pharaoh Necho II of Egypt had a brilliant idea. Rather than build a canal through the desert, to link the Red Sea to the Mediterranean – that idea had to wait until 1859 when the Suez Canal was built, which cut thousands of kilometres off the voyage – he decided to sail right around Africa, from the east coast of Egypt to the north. Which was all very well but he had absolutely no idea just how big Africa was! He couldn't make the trip himself, what with ruling and what not. So he hired some sailors from nearby Phoenicia, complete with their own boats. And off they went. It wasn't long before they wished that they'd never heard of nutty Necho and his potty plan. It took one gruelling year to sail down the east coast of Africa, and another to sail up the west coast – a round trip of 25,000 kilometres. And then when they got back no one believed they'd really made it!

TWO YEARS AND NOT ONE POSTCARD, YOU'LL HAVE TO DO BETTER THAN THAT!

The globe-trotting Greeks

They weren't the only ones to feel fed up. Nobody believed the Greek explorer, Pytheas, either, when he got back from his sailing trip in the north Atlantic. People laughed when he said he'd seen seas covered in ice. "Don't be daft," they sniggered. "You don't get ice at sea." (Bit of a Titanic error, that one!) The year was 304 BC. Poor Pytheas. To make matters worse, nobody believed he'd sailed round Britain either (where?), although he described its "extremely chilly climate"! He spent the rest of his life trying to convince people he was telling the truth.

Who really discovered America?

Despite warnings that he'd fall off the edge of the world or be eaten alive by sea monsters, Christopher Columbus set sail from Spain in 1492 to discover America. He didn't mean to discover America. He was actually looking for a new route to Asia and he firmly believed that he'd found one. (In fact, he'd miscalculated the size of the Earth and made it a quarter too small. He obviously didn't allow for sea floor spreading. Remember that?) He even made his crew swear to go along with his story and say that America was Asia. Else he'd have their tongues cut out!

Some horrible geographers agree with Columbus. They don't think he 'discovered' America either. In fact, they lined up several other suspects who they thought had beaten him to it. These included:

Luckily for Columbus, no one's been able to find convincing proof for any of these claims. So it looks like you're stuck with Columbus. Who must have been really pleased when his newly-found continent was named after his friend, Amerigo Vespucci, Italian navigator, sailor and ex-pickle-seller.

In 1519, another ace explorer, Ferdinand Magellan, had a dream. To sail around the world. No one had ever done this before! Would he make it? Read on to find out…

The amazing adventures of Ferdinand Magellan (circa 1480–1521)

Hardship on the high seas

1 Spain, August 1519. With five fine ships and a motley 280-man crew, Magellan sets out on the journey of a lifetime.

2 The Atlantic, August–December 1519. The ships head west. Apart from stores and supplies, they take thousands of combs, mirrors, small brass bells and fish hooks to trade for food and safe passage.

3 Rio de Janeiro, December 1519. They stop off for two weeks in Rio where the sailors are treated like gods. For some reason, they don't want to leave.

4 February 1520. After weeks and weeks of sailing around getting nowhere, the choice is this – to go back to Rio for a rest? Or sail south to the Southern Ocean, then head west? Magellan votes to carry on. Not a very popular move.

5 Along the South American coast, March 1520. After another month of freezing cold weather and storms, things turn even nastier. Three ships mutiny. Magellan has two ringleaders beheaded, and the other marooned. That should teach 'em.

6 A bit further along the South American coast, October 1520. One ship is lost and another deserts, taking a third of the stores.

7 At the tip of South America, October 1520. Magellan discovers a channel which links the Atlantic to the perilous Pacific … he calls it the Straits of Magellan – big head! It takes 38 days to sail through.

8 The Pacific, October 1520–March 1521. Things go from bad to worse. There's been no sight of land for months. And the sailors are struck down by scurvy*, starvation and thirst.

*Note: A disease caused by not eating your greens. So watch it!

9 The Philippines, March 1521. At last, land ahoy. And the end of the line for mad old Magellan. He is caught poking his nose into a local war, and killed. One ship is abandoned. Two sail on.

10 The Moluccas, November 1521. At the famous Spice Islands (Indonesia), the ships load up with valuable cloves. Disaster strikes as one ship springs a leak and sinks.

11 The Indian Ocean, February–July 1522. The fifth and last ship, *Victoria*, sails on. Her captain is Juan Sebastian del Cano, a former mutineer. Times are tough. The food goes off in the heat; the water turns yellow and scummy. The ships' masts are snapped by storms.

12 Spain, September 1522. Three long years and 94,000 kilometres later, *Victoria* limps home, a total wreck. Of the original crew of 280, only 18 survive to tell the tale. At least they can boast that they're the very first people to sail around the world.

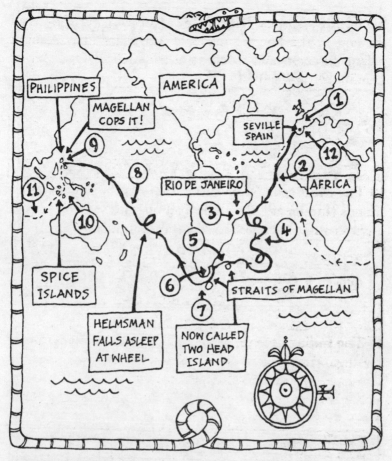

Latest equipment for explorers – hurry while stocks last!

Modern explorers are delving deeper than ever before. But they don't do the hard work themselves. Oh, no. Sometimes they don't even get their feet wet. They have lots of mod cons to help them out. Go on, give yourself a break. Meet Gloria, Jason, Kaiko and the gang. Check out these adverts…

OCEAN SUPPLIES CATALOGUE

THE GEOLOGICAL LONG-RANGE INCLINE ASDIC (DEEP OCEAN SURVEY SYSTEM)

GLORIA

A BIT OF A MOUTHFUL BUT YOU KNOW IT MAKES SENSE

Is mapping the sea floor getting you down? Having problems locating that missing oil, gas, fish?

FOR ALL YOUR DEEP-SEA SURVEYING NEEDS TRY

GLORIA THE LATEST WORD IN LONG-RANGE SIDE-SCAN SONAR

8m

SCAN

8 OUT OF 10 OWNERS SAID THEIR SCIENTISTS PREFER IT

EVER WONDERED WHAT IT LOOKS LIKE INSIDE THE WRECK OF THE TITANIC?

☆ WELL WONDER NO MORE! ☆

WITH THIS FABULOUS NEW VIDEO

TITANIC THE INSIDE STORY

BUY YOUR COPY WHILE STOCKS LAST

BRING A REAL WRECK INTO YOUR LIVING ROOM!

YOU CAN FIND OUT WITHOUT LEAVING YOUR ARMCHAIR!

NEW RELEASE

NEW

USING THE LATEST DEEP-SEA TECHNOLOGY, THESE ASTONISHING PICTURES ARE BROUGHT TO YOU BY JASON JUNIOR

A ROVING ROBOT

.R.O.V. REMOTE OPERATED VEHICLE

OPERATING INSTRUCTIONS: TAKE THE VIDEO OUT OF THE BOX AND SLOT IT IN YOUR VIDEO MACHINE. OBVIOUSLY!

THIS WEEK'S SPECIAL OFFER

DEEP FLIGHT 1

BACK BY POPULAR DEMAND
THE ONE PERSON SUBMERSIBLE (MINI-SUB)

BUY THIS MONTH AND GET A FREE PAIR OF TRENDY SECOND-HAND FLIP-FLOPS

THE SUB THAT'S NO TUB

TURN THE PAGE FOR DETAILS ⇒

WITH DEEP FLIGHT 1 YOU DON'T JUST SKIM THE SURFACE, YOU 'FLY' UNDERWATER DOWN TO DEPTHS OF ONE KILOMETRE...

OPERATING INSTRUCTIONS: SIMPLY STRAP YOUR-SELF IN, SWITCH ON THE CONTROLS... AND YOU'RE OFF!

COMING SOON...

DEEP FLIGHT 2...

DIVE 10 TIMES DEEPER, TO REACH PARTS OF THE DEEP-SEA NEVER REACHED BEFORE, STILL ON THE DRAWING BOARD... **BUT NOT FOR LONG!**

NEW FROM JAPAN

KAIKO*

WE ARE PLEASED TO INTRODUCE OUR BRAND NEW ROBOT PROBE. IT HAS DIVED AN AWESOME 10,911.4 METRES INTO THE MURKY MARIANAS TRENCH.

(JUST 60 cm SHORT OF **TRIESTE'S** WORLD RECORD)

THIS REMARKABLE MACHINE HAS THREE COLOUR, AND ONE BLACK-AND-WHITE VIDEO CAMERAS, A TV CAMERA AND A STILLS CAMERA

OPERATING INSTRUCTIONS: SIMPLY TIE KAIKO TO ITS LAUNCHER (CABLE INCLUDED), THEN ATTACH THE LAUNCHER TO YOUR SUPPORT SHIP, AND LAUNCH! DATA WILL BE SENT BY CABLE, VIA THE LAUNCH, TO THE SHIP

* KAIKO - SATISFACTION GUARANTEED - OR YOUR MONEY BACK (ALL £ 35 MILLION OF IT!)

Joshua Slocum – going it alone

One man who'd have found these mod cons far too newfangled was Captain Joshua Slocum, the first person to sail solo around the world. (Even though he couldn't swim.) Here's how he might have described his adventures in his diary:

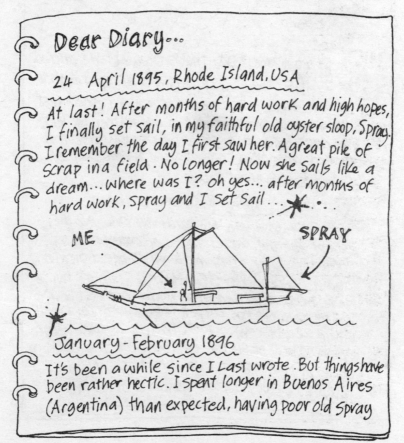

Dear Diary...

24 April 1895, Rhode Island. USA

At last! After months of hard work and high hopes, I finally set sail, in my faithful old oyster sloop, Spray. I remember the day I first saw her. A great pile of scrap in a field. No longer! Now she sails like a dream... where was I? oh yes... after months of hard work, spray and I set sail...✳·..

ME ➔

SPRAY ➔

January - February 1896

It's been a while since I last wrote. But things have been rather hectic. I spent longer in Buenos Aires (Argentina) than expected, having poor old Spray

113

restocked and refitted. In January we set off again, heading for the Straits of Magellan. What a journey! Battered by one storm after another. Waves like you've never seen before, seas the colour of thunder. I thought ✱ we'd had it, I can tell you. I just had

thunderous waves

time to drop the sails and batten down the hatches, when the storm hit like a cannon shot!

But Spray came good, that's my girl! We entered the straits on 11 February and dropped anchor in Chile three days later, for a well-earned rest. Lovely people, strange line in gifts; when we left five days later, they showered us with biscuits, smoked venison, a compass and several bags of...

Carpet tacks!

20 February 1896 (my birthday)

Fifty two again. No cards. No cake. No gifts. Except for the carpet tacks, of course!

some time later I never want to see a pirate again. Verminous SCUMBAGS! That's twice we've been attacked in as many months! If it hadn't been for the carpet tacks, goodness knows where we'd be now. I took the precaution, before going to bed, of sprinkling them over the deck. Howls of pain woke me up at midnight. Next thing I knew, a great bearded brute was standing in front of me, bold as brass. It was Black Pedro himself, the scourge of the straits. Now, he may think he looks big, bad and ugly but I wasn't scared of him. Oh no. I pointed my gun at him, sneered (really quite nastily) and he ran off!

GRR!

He turned up again next day, wanting to borrow my gun to shoot birds.

Do I look like I was born yesterday? Instead I gave him a knife for carving canoes, (a nice, safe, occupation) and sat down to a hot bowl of venison stew. There's nothing like a hot meal after a difficult day.

April-May 1896

Things couldn't be better; with Black Pedro behind us, and the weather turning warmer, we spent a happy two weeks on the island of Juan Fernandez (off the Chilean coast). As I headed ashore, some local people came aboard. I offered them coffee and doughnuts, in case they were peckish. The doughnuts went down well, so well in fact, that I made a tidy sum in gold showing the locals how to bake them. A most pleasant place.

six months later

I shan't bore you with more tales of storms and torn sails, though there's been plenty of both. Having crossed the Pacific and Indian Oceans, we spent some days on the island of St Helena (in the South Atlantic) where the governor treated me like a long lost friend. As I was leaving he gave me a gift, to keep me company, he said and handed me a... GOAT! Worse than any pirate or storm, it chewed through its rope, my best sun hat, it also

ate my charts and didn't give me a minute's peace. When we reached Ascension Island some weeks later, I put the wretched creature ashore and carried on alone. Bliss!

— Hooray!

STILL CHEWING!

3 July 1898

Journey's end. Three long years and 140,028 km later, Spray and I reached home. What I'll do now, I have no idea. Certainly goat-keeping's out of the question. Perhaps I'll write a book...

J. Slocum

And this is what Joshua Slocum did. His epic account of his record-breaking voyage, *Sailing Alone Around the World*, became a bestseller. He spent the next ten years writing and giving lectures. People often asked why he'd gone in the first place but he was never quite sure of the answer. In 1909, he was off again, planning to sail down the Amazon River. He was never seen again.

Deepish deep-sea diving

If you want to explore the sea by yourself, the best thing to do is go diving. My advice for beginners would be to start off small with a snorkel and flippers. And don't freak out if you come face-to-face with a fish. It's probably far more frightened of you.

Apart from exploring, we divers also suss out shipwrecks, search for sunken treasure, take recordings and measurements, monitor wildlife, and do fiddly jobs, like repairing old oil rigs. But there is a bit of a problem. The longest people can dive for, just by holding their breath, is a paltry two minutes 45 seconds. Any longer and you'd starve your brain of oxygen, which could damage it. And that means you can only go a few metres down. To dive any deeper, you need to take an air supply with you. We scuba-divers strap tanks of air on our backs and breathe through a mouthpiece. (By the way, to be a scuba-diver, you'll need to take lessons first. You can't just plunge in, flippers first. Ask at your local swimming-pool.) Breathing ordinary air (mostly oxygen and nitrogen), you can dive to about 50 metres. Breathing a different mixture of gases (oxygen, nitrogen and helium – that's the gas used to fill airships), you can dive deeper, to about 300 metres. But...

Horrible health warning!

If you surface too quickly after a dive, you may suffer horrible pains in your joints. These are called the "bends". They happen because the sudden change in pressure makes the nitrogen in the air you breathe form tiny bubbles in your blood like when you open a bottle of pop. If the bubbles reach your brain or spine, they can kill you. To avoid the bends, divers spend time in a "decompression chamber" where they return to surface pressure slowly and safely.

Cool clothes for deep-sea diving

Sadly, people aren't naturally nautical. To stay underwater for any length of time, we need all sorts of special clothes and equipment. Let me tell you how I pick the best diving gear for the job.

I'm about to dive into my first-ever modelling assignment. I tried three different diving suits – here are the pics, and my notes which tell you what I thought about each one.

Odious outfit No. 1

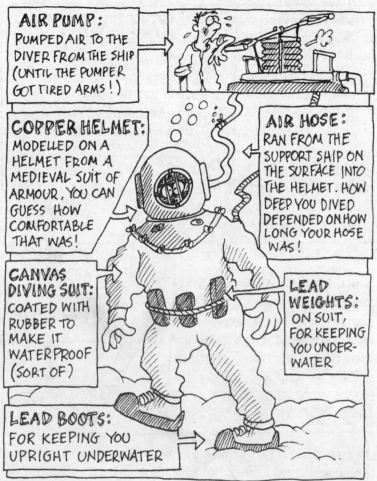

AIR PUMP: PUMPED AIR TO THE DIVER FROM THE SHIP (UNTIL THE PUMPER GOT TIRED ARMS!)

COPPER HELMET: MODELLED ON A HELMET FROM A MEDIEVAL SUIT OF ARMOUR, YOU CAN GUESS HOW COMFORTABLE THAT WAS!

AIR HOSE: RAN FROM THE SUPPORT SHIP ON THE SURFACE INTO THE HELMET. HOW DEEP YOU DIVED DEPENDED ON HOW LONG YOUR HOSE WAS!

CANVAS DIVING SUIT: COATED WITH RUBBER TO MAKE IT WATERPROOF (SORT OF)

LEAD WEIGHTS: ON SUIT, FOR KEEPING YOU UNDERWATER

LEAD BOOTS: FOR KEEPING YOU UPRIGHT UNDERWATER

My verdict: Horribly heavy and cumbersome. Almost impossible to walk in or even stand upright. And what if my air hose got tangled up or broken? I could easily be strangled or suffocated. It doesn't bear thinking about.
Marks out of 10: 0

Odious outfit No. 2

AQUALUNG: PORTABLE AIR TANK, STRAPPED TO MY BACK. ALSO CALLED **SCUBA:** (SELF-CONTAINED UNDER-WATER BREATHING APPARATUS

FACE MASK: KEEPS OUT WATER AND HELPS ME TO SEE BETTER

SNORKEL: FOR BREATHING AIR NEAR THE SURFACE

MOUTHPIECE: SHOULD FIT SNUGLY

WET SUIT: AN ALL-IN-ONE WATERPROOF RUBBER SUIT. SEALED AT THE EXTREMITIES. YOU CAN WEAR THERMAL UNDIES FOR EXTRA WARMTH. **OR DRY SUIT:** EVEN WARMER. FOR DIVING IN COLDER WATER. YOU CAN SLIP THIS ONE ON OVER YOUR ORDINARY CLOTHES AND STEP OUT BONE DRY

WEIGHT BELT: FULLY ADJUSTABLE

FLIPPERS OR FINS: FOR THAT EXTRA KICK

My verdict: This is more like it. It's lovely and light, and extremely comfortable. No problems of tangled hoses here. I think it rather suits me, don't you? Just bear in mind that it takes a while to learn to use an aqualung and to regulate the flow of air. Otherwise you could get yourself in serious trouble.

Marks out of 10: 8½

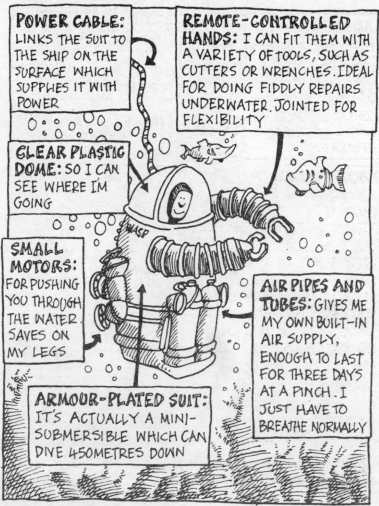

POWER CABLE: LINKS THE SUIT TO THE SHIP ON THE SURFACE WHICH SUPPLIES IT WITH POWER

REMOTE-CONTROLLED HANDS: I CAN FIT THEM WITH A VARIETY OF TOOLS, SUCH AS CUTTERS OR WRENCHES. IDEAL FOR DOING FIDDLY REPAIRS UNDERWATER. JOINTED FOR FLEXIBILITY

CLEAR PLASTIC DOME: SO I CAN SEE WHERE I'M GOING

SMALL MOTORS: FOR PUSHING YOU THROUGH THE WATER SAVES ON MY LEGS

AIR PIPES AND TUBES: GIVES ME MY OWN BUILT-IN AIR SUPPLY, ENOUGH TO LAST FOR THREE DAYS AT A PINCH. I JUST HAVE TO BREATHE NORMALLY

ARMOUR-PLATED SUIT: IT'S ACTUALLY A MINI-SUBMERSIBLE WHICH CAN DIVE 450 METRES DOWN

My verdict: Wow! They don't come much smarter than this, do they? This is an absolute must for the serious diver. I love the hands. A bit pricey for me, but a pleasure to wear.
Marks out of 10: 10

Whatever you're wearing, while you're dabbling about underwater, don't forget to have a good look around. Go on, the fish won't bite. On second thoughts, some of them might. You'll need to keep your wits about you. Are you all togged up and ready to jump? Good luck – you're about to meet some of the fishiest creatures on the planet...

DEEP, DARK AND ... DANGEROUS

There are thousands of creatures in the oceans. But are they all as scary as you'd expect them to be? The answer is: well, some of them are. Others are even bigger and scarier than you'd imagine. Of course, size isn't everything. Some of the deadliest sea creatures are horribly small. And some of the biggest wouldn't hurt a fly. Take, for example, a big blue whale...

Ten reasons to give a blue whale a wide berth

1 Blue whales are the biggest animals that have ever lived. Ever! Bigger than dinosaurs! Over 30 metres long and 130 tonnes in weight (that's as heavy as 20 elephants). More like a submarine than a sea mammal.

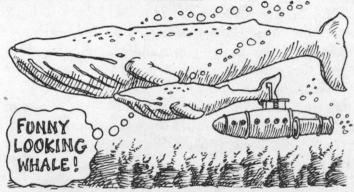

FUNNY LOOKING WHALE!

2 A blue whale's tongue weighs three whole tonnes. (As much as a whole rhinoceros.) Luckily, the blue whale has got a very big mouth!

3 Blue whale blubber (that's the thick layer of fat under its skin) can weigh 30 tonnes. It keeps the whale warm, especially in the parky polar seas, and gives it a streamlined shape for swimming.

4 Even baby blues weigh two tonnes at birth. And they grow up unbelievably fast. By the time they're two, they weigh a whopping 50 tonnes.

5 Blue whales have very big eyes compared to ours, about the size of footballs. We don't know how well they can see with them, though.

6 In the wild, blue whales can live for 80–90 years. If they're left to get on with it. But tens of thousands have been hunted and killed for their meat, blubber and whalebone, so that at one time they almost disappeared altogether. Today, though, they're making a comeback.

7 Blue whales couldn't survive on land. They're just too bloomin' big. They'd need such huge legs that they'd never be able to walk. The only place that can support their great bulk is the sea...

8 They might have lived on land once, though. Some whales and dolphins did. But they took to the sea about 50 million years ago in search of food. Here's how they became suited for swimming ...

- their bodies became streamlined

- their front legs became flippers

- their back legs disappeared

- their nostrils became blow-holes on top of their heads

- their hair was replaced by blubber.

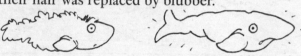

9 Instead of teeth, blue whales have huge, bony fringes hanging down the sides of their mouths. They use these like gigantic sieves for straining krill from the water.

10 And blue whales are BIG eaters. They eat tonnes of krill (see page 48) every day. So what would happen if you came face to face with one? Well, the answer is, nothing. Blue whales may be huge, but they're not interested in you ... not when there's lip-smacking krill to gorge on!

Whopping whale sharks

So, if the blue whale isn't dangerous, what is? The biggest fish in the sea, perhaps? Wrong! The whopping great whale shark may be 18 metres long, measure several metres around its middle and weigh about 20 tonnes (that's four largish elephants). It also has the thickest skin of any living creature, as tough and leathery as rubber. And it has absolutely no sense of danger. Which is why it bashes into boats. But deadly? No. Colliding with boats is about as dangerous as the whale shark gets. In fact, this huge fish is completely harmless, and so easygoing that it will even let divers ride on its back. With skin that thick, it can't feel a thing anyway!

I WANT TO GET OFF AT THE NEXT STOP

A short, shark, shock!

OK, so whales and whale sharks won't get you, but there's bound to be something that will?

Picture the scene. One minute you're splashing about in the sea, minding your own business, and the next ... you're on the menu for a hungry shark's lunch. A bit of an exaggeration? Or is it? Just how blood–curdling are these creatures? Is it really safe to go back into the water?

A shark's most fearsome features are its teeth. The gruesome great white has hundreds of spine-chilling choppers, as long as steak knives and razor sharp. This deadly hunter could easily bite you clean in two... Even dead, a shark can bite back. In 1977, an Australian fisherman was involved in a car crash. He was thrown on to the teeth of a dead shark's jaws, which happened to be lying on the back seat, and needed 22 stitches in his wounds! Ouch!

WANTED!

NAME: GREAT WHITE SHARK

KNOWN ALIASES: WHITE DEATH, WHITE POINTER, BLUE POINTER, MAN EATER.

KNOWN HAUNTS: ALL TROPICAL AND TEMPERATE SEAS

VITAL STATISTICS: LENGTH 6 METRES, WEIGHT 3 TONNES, TEETH 12cm LONG

KNOWN CRIMES: KILLS ABOUT 100 PEOPLE A YEAR

MODE OF OPERATION: CAN SMELL BLOOD A MILE AWAY

Not surprising when two-thirds of its brain is used for smelling. Then it sneaks up at high speed. Once it's got you in its sights, it opens its mouth and rolls back its eyes to protect them from damage. Then it sinks its teeth into you.

WEAPONS: TEETH – ABOUT 3,000 OF THEM, ARRANGED IN ROWS. WHEN ONE ROW WEARS OUT, THE ROW BEHIND SIMPLY SLIDES INTO PLACE. EASY.

WARNING!

THIS FISH IS ARMED AND DANGEROUS
DO NOT APPROACH AT ANY COST...

...YOU HAVE BEEN WARNED

127

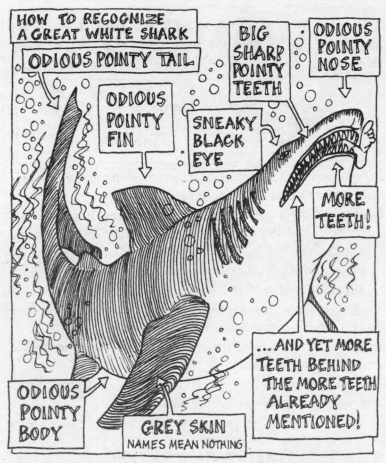

HOW TO RECOGNIZE A GREAT WHITE SHARK

ODIOUS POINTY TAIL

BIG SHARP POINTY TEETH

ODIOUS POINTY NOSE

ODIOUS POINTY FIN

SNEAKY BLACK EYE

MORE TEETH!

ODIOUS POINTY BODY

GREY SKIN
NAMES MEAN NOTHING

...AND YET MORE TEETH BEHIND THE MORE TEETH ALREADY MENTIONED!

Ten ways to avoid being snapped up by a shark

1 Wear a stripy swimming costume. With any luck, the shark will think you're a deadly stripy sea snake and leave you well alone.

2 Wear a stainless steel swimming suit, specially designed for the job. It's called a neptunic. It's made of thousands of metal rings. You might have some bruises but you won't get bitten.

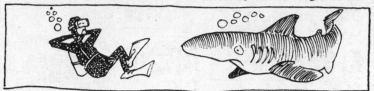

3 If you've even the tiniest cut or graze, don't go swimming. Sharks have a very sharp nose for blood…

4 Swim strongly with good, regular strokes. If you splash about weedily, a shark will think you're injured and eat you.

5 Try to startle the shark into submission. Slap the surface of the water and shout. It may not work but it'll keep you busy.

6 Don't swim alone. Sharks don't like company.

7 If you've got a shark after you, try to turn sharply and shake it off. They aren't as nimble as they look.

8 Don't swim at night, dawn or dusk. This is when most sharks are out and about.

9 If you're in a boat, try not to be seasick. The smell (and taste) of sick is irresistible to sharks.

10 And finally, great news for girls. Sharks are 13 times more likely to attack men than women!

But it's not just big creatures you need to beware of. Many smaller ones can hide a nasty surprise up their tentacles...

THE DAILY GLOBE'S
FISHERMAN'S FRIEND
Your questions answered

Dear Fisherman (or woman),
Hello, again. Fred here, your faithful fisherman's friend. It's been a funny old week, and no mistake. Me mailbag's been bursting at the seams. I'll try to get through as many letters as possible. But bear with me if I don't get round to yours. To tell you the truth, I've been having some bother with me bathypelagic cnidarians*. Playing me up something rotten they are. Right, then, here goes...

Dear Fred,
someone gave me a cone shell for christmas and it's proving a real pain to train
What can I do?

Fred replies: Blimey, you've got a job on your hands. You see, training's the least of your problems. These little beauties don't like being messed about with.

(*Roughly translated: Sea animals such as sea anemones and jellyfish that live at depths of between 1,000–4,000 metres down.)

Watch yourself, if you pick one up. You'll get a lethal dose of poison from a harpoon-like tooth, just under its shell. You won't have time to teach it to sit or stay. Within minutes, you won't be able to walk, speak or even breathe. A few hours later, you'll be dead, I'm afraid. I should take it back to the shop.

Dear Fred,
My little brother says that if i keep nicking his trainers, he'll put octopus spit in my tea. Should i be scared? (Ps please don't tell my parents i wrote in, im meant to be doing my geography homework.)

Fred replies: You young people, I don't know. Wasn't like that in my day. Still, I don't suppose it will hurt just this once. Where was I? Oh, yes, well, it all depends on what sort of octopus your brother uses. If it's a blue-ringed octopus, you're in trouble. This little creature kills more people a year than man-eating sharks. Its spit, in particular, is horribly poisonous. If I were you, I'd save up me pocket money and buy me own pair of trainers instead.

★ STAR LETTER ★

The writer of this week's star letter wins a day out with Fred on his sturdy old boat, *The Selfish Shellfish*. (If you get seasick, you'll have to make do with a signed photo instead.)

DEAR FRED,
IF A PERSON (NOT ME) WANTED TO MURDER SOMEONE (WHICH OF COURSE, THEY DON'T), IS THERE ANYTHING IN THE SEA THEY COULD USE?

Fred replies: Now, let me think. Bit of a fishy sort of question, this one. You could use Portuguese man-of-war tentacles. They're good and poisonous, I happen to know. I read somewhere, I forget where it was now, that they were once used in a murder attempt. Made into a soup, I believe they were. But the victim had a strong stomach and pulled through. Feeding someone to a shark would probably be quicker, if you ask me.

Dear Fred,
I can't tell me stones from me fish, can you help?

Fred replies: I know how you feel. It's a tricky one, this. Normally, stones look like stones and fish look like fish. But there is one very nasty exception. A stonefish looks like a stone and acts like a stone, until you tread on it... *Then* it spears you with its poisonous spines, perishin' thing. You'll be ranting and raving, you won't be able to help yourself. Then you'll be in pain like you've never felt before, and then you'll drop dead. If you're lucky. I should steer well clear, if I was you.

Dear Fred,
Yesterday I trod on a stingray. My leg's gone all blue and lumpy. Will it fall off?

Fred replies: It might, you know. I should get yourself off to the doctor. You see, the spike at the end of a stingray's tail is loaded with poison. What on Earth were you doing to get it so upset? You must have pestered it rotten for it to lash out like that. Stingrays like a quiet life, usually. By the way, if you've still got the spike, you could always turn it into a letter opener. People do, I'm told.

Dear Fred,
The lads and I have been having a bet on which is the deadliest creature in the sea? We just can't seem to agree, I say the tuna fish but the others just laugh. Can you settle things once and for all?

Fred replies: The tuna fish? Don't talk daft. But mind you, it could turn nasty if you were a small, tasty fish. Then you'd be lovely for lunch. But the most dangerous sea creature is the sea wasp jellyfish. It's small but deadly, and could kill you in a few minutes flat. Its tentacles ooze poison (enough in one jellyfish to kill 60 people). And it's so sneaky and see-through, you might not even notice it until it's too late. And that's not just my opinion. Ask anyone.

You could, for example, ask two scientists whose life's work was to study these odious creatures. And not always from a safe distance.

Killers down under

A pier off the coast of Australia, summer 1977

The scientists peered into the dark water along the edge of the pier. At last, they had found what they were looking for. There, bobbing and shimmering in the glare of the floodlights, were two ghostly shapes, with strings of ghastly tentacles streaming out behind their boxlike bodies. They were face to face with the infamous *Chironex fleckeri* (Latin for 'old bendy hand'). That's a sea wasp to you. The most venomous creature in the sea. This was the moment they had been waiting for.

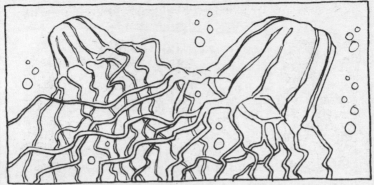

But how were they going to catch the killer jellyfish? If you're stung by a sea wasp, you can kiss goodbye to any thoughts of Christmas presents. You may not be there to open them. First, there's the unbearable pain, followed by problems breathing. Your heart stops pumping. In four minutes or less, unless you get treatment, you're dead. So, why on Earth try to catch this dastardly duo? Why not leave well alone, and go and study something else less sinister?

No. These were scientists on a mission – to capture a fully-grown sea wasp (which has a body the size of a basketball, only square, and 60-odd tentacles 5 metres long. Armed with masses of deadly stings). Besides, the scientists had a cunning plan. First, they had to cover up. They put on long trousers, long-sleeved shirts and gloves, taped tightly at the wrists. Then they grabbed some large plastic buckets and long-handled nets and set off for the pier. At first, everything went according to plan. Using the nets to push and shove, they coaxed the sea wasps into the buckets and hoisted them out of the water. So far, so good. Then disaster struck.

Catching the jellyfish was proving hot work and one of the scientists took his shirt off. BIG mistake. As he hauled a bucket out of the water, a single sea wasp tentacle was caught in the breeze and brushed ever so gently against his arm.

It was only the slightest, most glancing of touches – but the scientist felt as if his skin was on fire. An ugly, raw, red stripe snaked down his arm. And the pain! The pain was worse than anything he had ever known. But he was lucky. He had only been struck by a couple of centimetres of tentacle. It takes about three metres to be fatal. He didn't even want to think about that. And he didn't want to think about giving in either. Luckily, he pulled through.

Back at the lab the scientists took a close look at the sea wasp. No one had ever been this close. By looking at their beastly bodies, the scientists were going to be the first to find out how jellyfish live and breed – and, most importantly, examine their deadly poison. Information that could help to save lives.

DON'T PANIC! There are various things you can do if you're stung by a sea wasp. Which one would you think works best?

A DAB WITH VINEGAR	B DRINK ANTIVENOM	C WEAR TWO PAIRS OF TIGHTS

Answer: b) Your best option. But you need to act quickly and get to hospital fast. Antivenom is a medicine which stops venom (poison) working. It's injected into your muscles or veins and works almost immediately. By the way, a) can help in an emergency but you need to follow up with b). And c) isn't as silly as it sounds. Surfers entering sea wasp-infested waters sometimes wear two pairs of tights – one on their legs and one on their arms and heads – to protect them from jellyfish stings.

Dark doings deep down

OK, so most sea creatures aren't anything like as dangerous as sea wasps, but the places they live in can be deadly. For fish who live in the darkest depths of the sea, life can really get you down.

Not only is it…

Horribly cold – in the depths of the odious oceans, the water is f-f-freezing cold.

FOR THIS REASON MOST SEA CREATURES LIVE IN THE TOP 200 METRES OF WATER, WHERE IT'S WARM AND SUNNY

...and pitch black – when sunlight hits the sea, some bounces back into the sky and some is absorbed by the water. But it only reaches a short way down. Below about 250 metres, the water is black as night.

It's also...

Deeply depressing – the deeper you go underwater, the greater the weight of the water pressing down on you. For each ten metres you descend, the pressure increases by one kilogram per one square centimetre. It's crushing.

...and lonely – friendly faces are few and far between when you're a kilometre or more beneath the waves.

And it really is...

Very dangerous – there's not much food about down there so you have to watch your back. Deep-sea creatures eat worms, crustaceans and anything else they can get their teeth into. They also rely on the dead bodies of plants and animals raining down from above. These can take some time to reach them...

Despite all this, there are some odious ocean dwellers for whom these dangerous depths are home, sweet home. But how on Earth do they survive? Meet the distracting deep-sea angler fish...

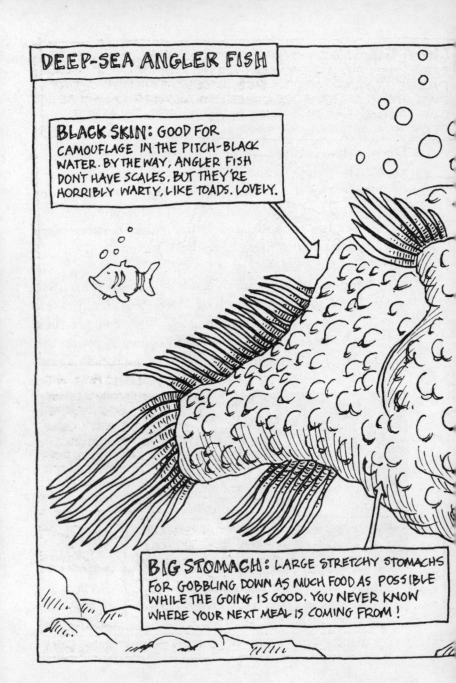

DEEP-SEA ANGLER FISH

BLACK SKIN: GOOD FOR CAMOUFLAGE IN THE PITCH-BLACK WATER. BY THE WAY, ANGLER FISH DON'T HAVE SCALES, BUT THEY'RE HORRIBLY WARTY, LIKE TOADS. LOVELY.

BIG STOMACH: LARGE STRETCHY STOMACHS FOR GOBBLING DOWN AS MUCH FOOD AS POSSIBLE WHILE THE GOING IS GOOD. YOU NEVER KNOW WHERE YOUR NEXT MEAL IS COMING FROM!

LIGHT BULB: YES, LIGHT BULB. HOW ELSE WOULD YOU SEE IN THE DARK? THE LIGHT BULB DANGLES OVER THE FISH'S MOUTH ON A LONG FIN LIKE A FISHING ROD. IT'S A BLOB, MADE UP OF MILLIONS OF TINY LIGHT-GIVING BACTERIA. THE ANGLER FISH ALSO USES ITS LIGHT AS BAIT. SMALL FISH MISTAKE IT FOR A SNACK AND SWIM TOWARDS IT. STRAIGHT INTO THE ANGLER'S MOUTH.

BIG MOUTH: HUGE AND LINED WITH NASTY LONG GNASHERS WHICH CURVE BACKWARDS. WHY? WELL THEY LET PREY IN, NICE AS PIE, THEN THEY SPRING FORWARD AND SLAM SHUT! LIKE A ROW OF PRISON BARS, SO THE PREY CANT GET OUT!

LUMPY BODY: ANGLER FISH DON'T HAVE SLEEK, STREAMLINED BODIES, LIKE OTHER FISH, BECAUSE THEY DON'T NEED TO SWIM FAST TO CATCH THEIR FOOD. IN FACT, THEY'RE REALLY RATHER FLABBY AND SLOW. SOME SPEND ALL DAY LYING AROUND ON THE SEABED, MOUTHS WIDE OPEN, WAITING FOR FOOD TO SWIM IN!

UT ANGLER FISH AREN'T THE ONLY FISH TO SEE IN THE DARK

How on Earth do they do it?

1 Over half of all deep-sea fish make their own light. Some glow because of chemical reactions inside their bodies. Others use clumps of bacteria as torches.

2 What do you think sea creatures use their lights for? To...

A FIND FOOD...

B FIND MATES...

C FIND THEIR WAY IN THE DARK...

D SCARE OFF ATTACKERS...

BEAT IT!

E TALK TO EACH OTHER...

DOT DOT DASH

DOT DASH DOT

Answer: All of these are true.

3 Flashlight fish have a light under each eye. They can turn them on and off by covering them up with shutters of skin, like tiny curtains. A handy trick for puzzling predators. The flashlights are bright enough to light up a small room. And they carry on glowing even after the fish has snuffed it.

4 Twinkle, twinkle, little seastar! Some seastars (they're related to starfish) glow green and blue as a warning to predators that they taste terrible.

5 Little firefly squid use their lights for camouflage and to get to know a mate. They also squirt enemies with luminous blue goo which gives them time to make a quick getaway. In Japan, fishermen bait their lines with slithers of these sparkling squid.

Earth-shattering fact
During the Second World War, Japanese sailors hit upon a way of saving electricity. They rubbed their hands with some luminous bacteria found inside shellfish. This gave just enough light to read top-secret files by, but not enough to alert enemy warships.

Armed and dangerous

In the depths of the ocean, it's a fish-eat-fish world. If you can't fight back, you'll soon go under. Many sea creatures are well-equipped for survival, with stings, sharp teeth, prickles and poison. Some are more cunning than others. Here are a few of the tricks they have tucked up their fins...

Sharp-shooter The no-nonsense pistol shrimp shoots its food down at close range. It simply takes aim ... and fires, snapping its right claw with a noise like gunshot. This sends shock waves racing through the water, stunning the victim while the shrimp moves in for the kill.

Getting the point Needlefish are long, thin, and extremely painful when pestered. A sailor in the USA was once pinned to his boat when a needled needlefish leapt out of the sea and stuck straight through his leg.

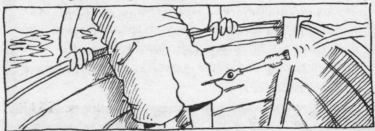

Second-hand poison Sea slugs don't have weapons of their own to protect them from being eaten. So they gobble down sea anemones, complete with stings, and use them instead. The anemones' stings pass through the sea slug's body and lie just under its skin. If a famished fish brushes past, the stings stick into it. Ouch!

A shocking tail The black torpedo ray stuns prey and predators by shocking them with electricity (made in its head). A fisherman in England once caught a torpedo ray and put it on display. He charged spectators a small fee to guess its weight. It made his fortune. No one could hold on to the ray for long enough to get a proper feel!

Armless fun

When a starfish wants to distract an attacker, it simply leaves an arm or two behind. Weird or what? Try this quick quiz to see what you know about the very strange starfish:

1 Starfish can have up to 40 arms. TRUE/FALSE?
2 Starfish don't have heads. TRUE/FALSE?
3 The biggest starfish ever found was the size of a dustbin lid. TRUE/FALSE?
4 Starfish spend their day mugging molluscs. TRUE/FALSE?
5 Starfish have terrible table manners. TRUE/FALSE?

Answers:
1 True. If a starfish loses an arm (see above), it just grows another one. What's more, it can grow a whole new body from a tiny piece of arm (though it takes a year or two). And mistakes can happen. Some starfish end up with four or 40 arms, instead of the usual five or six.
2 True. But they do have eyes on the ends of their arms. Because they don't have a head, they don't have a brain either! A starfish's body is basically just a mouth and stomach on legs (or arms).
3 False. The biggest starfish are actually twice as big as a

143

dustbin lid! They measure almost 1.5 metres across the tips of their arms. Yet their bodies are only 2.5 centimetres wide. The smallest starfish are a paltry 5 millimetres across. You could easily fit one on your thumbnail.

4 True. Under each arm, a starfish has a row of tiny suckers (called tube feet). When a starfish fancies a snack, it wraps its arms tightly around a mollusc so that it's stuck fast, prises it open, then gobbles it up.

5 True. The crown-of-thorns starfish is particularly bad. When it wants to crunch on a piece of coral, it sicks out its stomach over the coral, digests it slowly outside its body, then pulls its stomach in again. Disgusting! And if that's not bad enough, the crown-of-thorns is also the only poisonous starfish, packing a punch with its needle-sharp spines. They are currently eating their way through the Great Barrier Reef!

You can't blame a starfish for trying. The truth is, that, lovely or loathsome, prickly or poisonous, every single sea creature has something to fear. Even the big ones. But the greatest risk isn't from each other. It's much, much worse than that. There's one creature all fish should be scared of. Guess who?

SEA SICK

For centuries, humans have been using the oceans as a gigantic dustbin. It's true! The oceans are so huge, that tipping any old rubbish into the sea seemed quite a good way to lose it for ever. But every year, 26 billion tonnes of rubbish, sewage, old industrial chemicals, oil and even radioactive waste finds its way into the salty sea. And it's all still there, somewhere. No wonder it's making the sea sick. All this pollution has a fatal effect on sea animals and plants, too. It even has harmful effects on humans. And it's taking its toll on some of the most beautiful features of the sea.

Coral reefs at risk

If it's life and colour you're after, visit a coral reef. The busiest places in the big, blue sea. The biggest can grow as large as islands, yet they're built by creatures no larger than ants. And they're dying. Over 10 per cent of reefs have gone already and another 60 per cent are seriously sick. But why on Earth do coral reefs matter? Try this quiz to find out more. Better still, try it out on someone else, your mum, dad, teacher…

Coral conundrum

1 What on Earth is coral made from?
a) rocks
b) animals
c) plants

2 How many of these creatures are at home on a coral reef?
a) lionfish
b) giant clams
c) moray eels
d) clownfish
e) butterfly fish
f) feather stars
g) reef sharks
h) parrot fish
i) sea snakes
j) nudibranchs

3 Where on Earth do parrot fish sleep?
a) on the seabed
b) on a coral ledge
c) in a sleeping-bag

4 How fast does a coral reef grow?
a) about 5 millimetres a year
b) about 2.5 centimetres a year
c) about 1 kilometre a year

5 Where on Earth are most coral reefs found?
a) in the Pacific Ocean
b) in the Atlantic Ocean
c) in the Indian Ocean

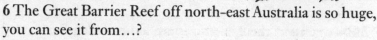

6 The Great Barrier Reef off north-east Australia is so huge, you can see it from…?
a) the moon
b) New Zealand
c) south-west Australia

7 Which of these can be made from coral?
a) teeth
b) eyes
c) bones

8 What on Earth is a coral atoll?
a) a coral island
b) a coral fish
c) a piece of coral shaped like a brain

9 Coral reefs are in danger from…?
a) souvenir collectors
b) oil exploration
c) pollution
d) fishing boats
e) cutting down trees on land

10 What on Earth can we do to save them?
a) dig them up and move them elsewhere
b) turn them into marine parks
c) build glass tanks around them

Answers:

1b) Scientists used to think coral was made from plants. In fact, coral reefs are built by tiny animals, called polyps. They're close relatives of the jellyfish and of sea anemones. They live together in groups of millions and millions. Coral is actually the hard, stony cases which the polyps build to protect their soft, squashy bodies, using chemicals from the water. Most of a reef is made of empty white cases (the polyps inside having long since died). But the colourful top layer is very much alive.

2 The answer is all of them. Coral reefs are teeming with life. In fact, they're home to so much sea life that they're known as the gardens of the sea. A third of all types of fish live among them with thousands of other cool creatures for company. Never heard of a nudibranch? It's a fancy name for a brightly-coloured sea slug. The colours are a warning: "Go away and leave me alone. I taste horrible!"

3c) The parrot fish has very strange sleeping habits. At night, it blows a sticky bubble of jelly around its body, like a sleeping-bag, then dozes off inside. Safe and snug from its enemies, like moray eels. They can't smell the parrot fish while it's in its bed.

4b) Coral grows at the same speed as your fingernails, about 2.5 centimetres a year. At this rate, a reef takes millions of years to grow. Scientists can date reefs by giving them X-rays, just like the ones doctors use to look at your insides. These show tiny rings on the polyps' coral cases. Each ring takes a year to grow. The Great Barrier Reef in Australia is at least 18 million years old.

5c) Over half of all coral reefs are in the Indian Ocean where conditions are perfect for the corals to grow. (There are also reefs in the Pacific and Atlantic.) Corals like warm, sunny and shallow waters best. If the sea level rises, or gets too cold, the coral gets sick and dies. Sunlight is vital. The polyps grow in partnership with tiny plants (algae) which help to glue the reef together. And algae need sunlight to make their food. If the water is dirty, this can also stunt the corals' growth.

6a) The Great Barrier Reef is over 2,000 kilometres long and covers over 200,000 square kilometres (that's twice the size of Iceland). It's the biggest coral reef in the world and the biggest structure made by any living things, including us. Wow!

7b) and c) Believe it or not, coral eye sockets and bones are already being fitted in humans. Coral is perfect for the job because its structure (it's full of tiny holes) is similar to real human bone. At present, though, only three of the 2,500 types of coral can be used to make body bits. These are found in the South Pacific where islanders already use coral to build everything from houses and jewellery to sewer pipes! Only a very small amount of coral – about enough to fill the boot of a car – is harvested each year for surgery. And it's removed very carefully so the reef isn't ruined.

8a) Coral atolls begin life as reefs growing on the slopes of volcanoes. Over the years, the volcanoes sink into the sea. But the coral keeps growing to form a horseshoe-shaped island around a sleepy lagoon. The Pacific Ocean is full of them. Heavenly for holidays!

CORAL

VOLCANO

HORSE SHOE RING

9 Sadly, the answer is all of these. Tonnes and tonnes of coral are stolen for jewellery, ornaments and for decorating people's aquariums. Reefs are blasted with explosives in the search for oil. They're also poisoned by pollution and smothered by soil which slops into the sea when trees are cut down on land. Fishing is a tricky problem. Millions of people rely on reef fish for their food. But fishing boats can smash up the coral as they dredge the reef for fish and shellfish.

10b) The good news is that, left well alone, coral reefs can recover. Some countries have turned their reefs into parks which are guarded day and night. Tourists and divers have to pay to visit and woe betide anyone caught taking bits home.

Horrible human habits

But we humans are still pretty horrible. If we want to make the sea really sick, we're going the right way about it. Here are just some of our sick habits...

1 Pump it

What we do: Pump stinking sewage straight into the sea. And let chemicals and pesticides from farms keep washing into the sea from our rivers.

What's so sick about that? Plankton (tiny plants) eat up the sewage and other chemicals, then it grows and grows. And grows. Until it covers the sea in thick, green slime. The sinister slime blocks out sunlight which other plants need to make food. And when it dies, it's eaten by bacteria which starve the water of oxygen, so fish and shellfish suffocate.

Why we won't stop: More than half the world's people live close to the coast, so it's the simplest way to wash away our waste and wash our hands of the problem.

2 Leak it

What we do: Leak poisonous metals, such as mercury and lead, into the sea from factories, mines and boats.

What's so sick about that? The metals are digested by fish, then move up the food chain until they reach people, with fatal effects. In the 1950s, hundreds of people in Japan suffered brain damage after eating fish that was poisoned with mercury. It had leaked into the sea from a nearby chemical factory.

Why we won't stop: Factories supply us with many of the things we use in our daily lives, from cars and food to nuts and bolts. And mines produce raw materials. People are now experimenting with cleaner ways of going about things but it's a long, slow process.

3 Dump it

What we do: Dump radioactive waste from nuclear power stations on land into the sea in a concrete case.

What's so sick about that? This waste is deadly poisonous. Even in its concrete case, it can take thousands of years to become safe. If it leaks into the water, it could cause cancer and other fatal diseases (in humans and sea animals).

Why we won't stop: Because we don't really know what else to do with it. Imagine the outcry if it was buried on land. Out of sight is out of mind.

4 Chuck it

What we do: Dump millions of tonnes of rubbish – plastic bags, bottles, oil drums, barrels, tins and ropes – into the sea every year. Five million tonnes of this is chucked over the sides of ships.

What's so sick about that? Thousands of sea birds, mammals, turtles and fish get caught up in old ropes and nets, and die as they try to escape. And piles of rubbish are washed up on beaches when the tide comes in. Now that's pretty sick!

Why we won't stop: We make so much rubbish that it can't all be disposed of on land. Already, billions of tonnes is buried underground. This is OK for rubbish that rots away, but plastics and metals last for ages. Basically, we need to throw away less rubbish, or recycle materials like plastic and glass. As for all those old ropes and nets, fishermen need to tidy up after themselves. Or else.

5 Spill it

What we do: Run oil-tankers aground and spill millions of litres of oil into the sea.

What's so sick about that? The oil clogs birds' feathers so they can't keep warm or stay afloat, and they die. Other sea creatures are poisoned when they try to swallow the oil. Some of the chemicals used to soak up the oil are even more dangerous. It can take years and years to clean up the mess.

Why we won't stop: Oil makes the world go round. It fuels our cars, factories, homes, you name it. But it's also a killer. Oil companies need to be more responsible – and, to be fair, many are trying. For example, some oil tankers are now made with double thickness walls to help prevent any leaks. But it all costs a great deal of money. Basically, we want cheap petrol so tankers are run cheaply.

6 Drill it

What we do: Pollute the sea with noise from ships, by drilling into the seabed and testing out new weapons under water.

What's so sick about that? Sound waves carry well underwater and many sea creatures have sensitive hearing. Imagine living in *that* din.

THEY'RE DRILLING FOR OIL IN THE GARDEN

Why we won't stop: We don't have to hear it, so we turn a deaf ear. Of course, it would be different if you were just about to drop off to sleep at night when someone started drilling into the pavement outside your window, wouldn't it?

Earth-shattering fact
The North Sea is now so disgustingly dirty that, in ten years' time, fish like mackerel, cod and haddock could be extinct. So enjoy those fish and chips ... while you still can.

ONE SKATE AND CHIPS

No wonder the sea's sick. Wouldn't you be?

Do we need the oceans more than they need us?

You can make up your own mind by reading about three of the things we wouldn't have without the odious oceans.

Rotten rain The oceans play a vital part in the weather. Here's what happens:

1 The sun warms up the oceans and millions of litres of water rises into the sky as (invisible) water vapour.

2 As the vapour rises, it cools and turns back into liquid water.

3 Then it falls as rain.

4 On land, rivers carry the water back into the sea.

5 Then the whole thing starts all over again.

HOT

NOT AGAIN!

You might think less rain would be a good thing. Then geography field trips wouldn't be so wet and soggy. Think again. Without the rain, no plants could grow, and without plants, there'd be no food. Oceans are also crucial for controlling the Earth's temperature, by absorbing and releasing heaps of heat and sharing it out more evenly.

Amazing oxygen Without the oceans, you wouldn't be able to breathe. The sea is full of tiny green plants, called algae, which make over half of all the oxygen we breathe. How? Well, algae don't need to go shopping for food. They make their own. They use sunlight to turn carbon dioxide (a gas) and water into food. And oxygen.

Tuna fish sandwiches Millions of people on Earth rely on the oceans for food. Not just tasty tuna fish but crabby crustaceans, meaty molluscs, seaweed, salt and so on. The problem is that so many fish are caught that stocks are running dangerously low. Talking of tuna, in the last 20 years, stocks of tuna in the West Atlantic have dropped by a massive 90 per cent. The chips are down.

Saving the sea

The seas have certainly ended up in a pretty sick state, but things aren't quite as gloomy as they sound. Campaigns are helping to make us all aware of the terrible state of affairs. 1997 was the International Year of the Reef. You could help out by adopting your own chunk of coral reef – you can adopt a whale, too, if you think you can cope!

1998 was officially the International Year of the Ocean. Governments all round the world were asked to clean up their acts and try to cut down on polluting the water and hauling too many fish from the sea. These efforts include international conventions to prevent pollution by aircraft and ships. It was also agreed that the best way to persuade people to save the sea was by encouraging them to get to know it better. It's too early to say yet whether this idea has worked. But there's still plenty of time for you to pop down to your nearest beach and make friends with the not-so-odious oceans.

HORRIBLE INDEX